POEMS AND SONGS,

MAISTLY SCOTCH,

BY

ANDREW WANLESS.

SECOND EDITION,

TO WHICH IS ADDED A NUMBER OF NEW PIECES NEVER BEFORE PUBLISHED

While the daisy decks the lea,
Scotia's sangs will never dee—
Floating down time's silent river,
Time and they will die together.

DETROIT, MICH.
PUBLISHED BY A. WANLESS, 133 JEFFERSON AVENUE.
1873.

Printed by THE DAILY POST COMPANY, Detroit, Mich.

PREFACE TO THE FIRST EDITION.

THE primary design in the composition of these "Poems and Songs" was an endeavor to link the present with the past—to recall the scenes of our early years—to bring up, in imagination, the braw lads and the bonnie lasses that we forgathered with in the days of the lang syne, and attempt to describe, on this side of the Atlantic, the wimpling burns, the gowany braes, the bonnie glens, the broomy dells, and the heather-clad mountains of our native land: the land where Wallace and Bruce wielded the patriotic sword, and where Ramsay, Burns, Scott, Tannahill, and many more sang the songs of love and liberty.

The secondary object was to lay before my countrymen and the American people some specimens of the Scottish vernacular. At the present time I am sorry to say that a number of poets are in the habit of losing themselves in the clouds, and instead of writing to be understood, one would naturally imagine that they try their best to mystify and befog the reader. In contradistinction I have attempted to keep as near the earth as possible, and endeavored to clothe my sentences in plain and home-spun attire. Some other poetasters, from their lack of wit, no doubt, have attempted to wring out bastard and weak puerility by mangling, distorting and misspelling the English language. These authors who thus pamper and pander to the vulgar taste, in my poor opinion are more to be pitied than despised.

No one that is conversant with the Scottish language can deny its rich beauty and its adaptation for lyric and descriptive composition. If I have failed to make this volume readable, the fault cannot be attributed to the language, but on the other hand the demerit must be laid at the door of the author.

A few of the "Poems and Songs" first appeared in the *Scottish American Journal*, *Hamilton Times*, *Sarnia Observer*, and the Detroit Daily Newspapers, to the respective editors of which I return thanks for courtesies extended. The majority of the pieces, I may however state, appear in this collection for the first time.

PREFACE TO THE SECOND EDITION.

THE success that attended the publication of the first edition of this work, has induced the author to issue a second edition, to which is added a number of "Poems and Songs," never before published. The first edition was more favorably reviewed by the press of the United States, Canada and Scotland, than the author, in his most sanguine moments, ever anticipated; and he trusts that this edition will also merit the favorable criticism of the press and the patronage of the public.

DETROIT, MICH., June 1873.

TABLE OF CONTENTS.

	PAGE
A Sabbath Morning in Scotland..	24
A Kittlin Clatter................	32
A Pastoral.....................	47
A Precious Jewel...............	68
A Word to the Canadian Weevil.	73
A Weak Man and a Strong Woman	137
A Reformation	139
A Scotch Sangster's Comin'	141
Aye keep your Heart Aboon.....	10
Belle Isle aboon Detroit..........	147
Bonnie Nell..........	155
Caledonian Games on Belle Isle..	43
Craigie Castle...................	143
Come, Sweetheart, come.........	159
Detroit is the Town for Me......	149
Ellen Dear.......	171
Folk should aye be equal Yokit..	52
Her Heart was all Mine Own....	146
Her love for me did Wither......	158
Hohenwindsor.......	65
Home Recollections.....	12
I ance had a lad................	176
I Lo'e my Alice best o' a'... . .	168
Jean and Donald	129
Jeanie Bell......................	150
Jineral O'Neil...................	151
Kate o' Boontree.......	161
Lamentation for Mike Gill.......	49
Lammermoor................ ...	165
Little Nellie.................. ..	157
Mary...........................	164
My Love, O! Come to Me......	148
Nan o' Lockermacus.........	87
Our Mither Tongue	9
Rob Trotter's Gimmer..........	57
Scottish Sangs..................	38
Tam and Tib............... ...	83
That's but Nat'ral...............	29
The Trysting Nicht	167
The Rose of Springwells.........	169
The Maid of Wayne............	170
The Flower o' Duntroon.........	172
The Death of McGregor.........	173
The Auld Man's Courtship.......	174
The Creelin'................... .	16
The Dialogue of the Breeks......	39
The Wallace Monument....	61
The Scott Centenary.............	66
The Cat Aneath the Chair.......	77
The Poor o' the Parish..........	105
The Second Sight................	111
The Wife and the Breeks...	126
The Men o' the Merse.....	153
The Banks o' the Dye...	154
The lang Tailor o' Whitby......	155
The Cow ave Chicago	156
The Courting o' the Widow.....	162
Tib's Slighted me ye ken.	124
To John A. Bruce...............	117
To Dad Brichan	108
To James Walker...............	106
To A. H. Wingfield.............	62
To James McKay...............	27
Too Much Liberty..............	71
Turning the Key................	20
War and Peace.................	31
When Nell was Aughteen........	175
Willy has proved false to me. ..	166
Who Should and Who Shouldn't..	121
Who's Comin'?	160
Ye Ballad of Jeanie Johnston	34
Proverbs	177
Glossary	187

TO THE MEMBERS

OF THE

St. Andrew's Societies and Caledonian Clubs

OF THE

UNITED STATES AND CANADIAN DOMINION

THIS VOLUME

IS MOST RESPECTFULLY DEDICATED

BY THE AUTHOR.

Our Mither Tongue.

Read before the St. Andrew's Society, Detroit, November 30, 1870.

IT'S monie a day since first we left
Auld Scotland's rugged hills—
Her heath'ry braes and gow'ny glens,
Her bonnie winding rills.
We lo'ed her in the by-gane time,
When life and hope were young,
We lo'e her still, wi' right guid will,
And glory in her tongue!

Can we forget the summer days
Whan we got leave frae schule,
How we gade birrin' down the braes
To daidle in the pool?
Or to the glen we'd slip awa
Where hazel clusters hung,
And wake the echoes o' the hills—
Wi' our auld mither tongue.

Can we forget the lonesome kirk
Where gloomy ivies creep?
Can we forget the auld kirk yard
Where our forefather's sleep?
We'll ne'er forget that glorious land,
Where Scott and Burns sung—
Their sangs are printed on our hearts
In our auld mither tongue.

Auld Scotland ! land o' mickle fame !
  The land where Wallace trod,
The land where heartfelt praise ascends
  Up to the throne of God !
Land where the Martyrs sleep in peace,
  Where infant freedom sprung,
Where Knox in tones of thunder spoke
  In our auld mither tongue !

Now Scotland dinna ye be blate
  'Mang nations crousely craw,
Your callants are nae donnert sumphs,
  Your lasses bang them a'.
The glisks o' heaven will never fade,
  That hope around us flung—
When first we breath'd the tale o' love
  In our auld mither tongue !

O ! let us ne'er forget our hame,
  Auld Scotland's hills and cairns,
And let us a' where'er we be,
  Aye strive "to be guid bairns" !
And when we meet wi' want or age
  A-hirpling owre a rung,
We'll tak' their part and cheer their heart
  Wi' our auld mither tongue.

AYE KEEP YOUR HEART ABOON.

Respectfully inscribed to A. D. Fraser, Esq.

OH ! monie a day has gane, guidfolks,
  Since first this warld I kent,
And folk o' a' degrees I've seen
  Gie way to discontent ;

They growl at this, they growl at that,
Their growlin's never doon,
They ne'er will learn to sing wi' me—
"Aye keep your heart aboon."

Aye keep your hearts aboon, guidfolks,
Whatever may befa',
O! ne'er forget the gowden words—
"Tine heart and ye tine a'."
The wimplin' burns, the bonnie birds,
A' nature sings the tune,
And tells the thankless race o' man
To keep their hearts aboon.

I no deny that we, guidfolks,
Ha'e a' our load o' care,
And e'en at times been on the brink
O' even-doon despair;
But we should mind that there was *ane*
Who bore the cross and croon,
Who taught us a' to live in hope,
And trust in heaven aboon.

Aye keep your hearts aboon, guidfolks,
And dinna be down cast,
There comes a blink o' sunshine aye
When angry winds blaw past.
'Tis best to turn our back on care,
For he's a cauldriff loon,
But Leddy Hope says to us a'
"Aye keep your hearts aboon."

Dame Nature ne'er design'd, guidfolks,
When first she ga'e us breath,
That we should stand in mortal fear
O' that grim Carl Death,

She ga'e us Hope and sister Joy,
To tend us late and soon,
Sae let us strive to be content,
And keep our hearts aboon.

Distress and grief will come, guidfolks,
But Pity aye draws near,
And Hope and Joy will watch and wait
To wipe the waefu' tear;
When winter's gane the spring will come,
And syne the flow'rs o' June,
The wells o' Hope they ne'er rin dry,
Sae keep your hearts aboon.

The days and years slip by, guidfolks,
And mingle with the past,
And Reason tells us, ev'ry breath
Draws nearer to the last,
And when Death comes, as sure he will,
Be comin' late or soon,
May Faith and Hope attendant wait
To waft our souls aboon.

Home Recollections.

Inscribed to D. Bethune Duffield, Esq.

MY Muse! Come flit with me an hour,
To gow'ny braes and sylvan dells;
Come fancy, dwell in Lammermoor—
Amang the bonnie heather-bells.

Let me forget the weary years,
The hardships and the ills that grieve me,
Let me forget the bygone tears,
Since I, in sorrow, laith did leave thee!

Your hills in lovely grandeur vie,
Your crystal streamlets rin sae clear,
Still let me trace the winding Dye,
And muse on hame and Scotia dear.

With eager step climb Redpath hill,
With rapture scan the rural shade,
And see the cot beside the rill,
Where first my infant footsteps stray'd.

I see our house, our auld, auld hame,
My brothers, sisters and the lave,
I see a form I scarce can name,
Who now lies mould'ring in the grave.

The falt'ring tongue of woe is weak,
To tell the soul's despairing gloom,
The silent tears alone can speak
The grief that's cradled in the tomb.

My Mother! thou wert kind to me,
Although the grave did early get thee,
The tear still rises in mine e'e,
My Mother! I will ne'er forget thee!

And there my other parent lies,
Set free from care and carking strife—
An honest man, sedate and wise,
As ever drew the breath of life.

There stands the school—the pathway gate,
Where aft my truant feet did climb,
Lur'd by the wand of luckless fate,
To weave unseen the rustic rhyme.

To wander by the murm'ring stream,
To pull the roses fresh and fair,
And learn to dream life's idle dream,
And build the castle in the air.

Ah me ! upon yon grassy glade,
Where high the clust'ring rowans hung,
How aft I've sat beneath the shade,
To list the notes the blackbird sung !

The golden cloud, the sunny beam,
Have melted into gloamin' grey ;
My playmates—lost upon life's stream—
E'en like a wave have passed away !

Down in the glen the churchyard lies,
The hazel bank the streamlet laves,
Yon aged willow soughs and sighs,
And weeps upon the lowly graves.

In fancy still I fondly stray,
And tread the path my fathers trod,
Where thorns and briars half hide the way
That leads up to the house of God.

My mem'ry conjures up the look,
The rev'rend Pastor's locks so grey,
I still can see him ope the book,
And hear the words : "Come, let us pray."

A stillness reigns in every aisle,
A gloomy and a holy calm—
Devotion hovers round the while,
And wafts to heaven the sacred Psalm.

With quiv'ring lip and tearful cheek
The Pastor speaks of God and love ;
Through Christ, the lowly and the meek,
He points the way to heaven above.

He tells of earth and earthly woe,
Of heaven and heaven's eternal day,
Where we shall God, our Father, know—
And all our tears be washed away !

The young and old attentive sit,
    With watchful eye and list'ning ear,
While o'er their face alternate flit—
    A heavenly hope, an earthly fear.

The vile he warns to think, to stop—
    The path to heaven is still the best;
To drooping hearts he counsels hope,
    To weary souls he speaks of rest.

The sunbeams glimmer through the trees,
    And dance above the solemn throng,
While borne upon the gentle breeze
    To heaven ascends the heartfelt song.

O, Scotland ! may the God of life
    Forever shower his blessings on thee !
O ! may the seeds of hate and strife,
    Be sown for never more upon thee !

And may thy sons be ever found
    An honor to the human race,
May God in his eternal round
    From thee and thine ne'er hide his face !

The bard nursed in the lap of care,
    Oppressed with grief and tangled fate—
His fleeting moments cry "prepare !"
    Time never shuts the church yard gate.

O ! may we never, ne'er forget
    The lessons of our early years;
Examples that our parents set,
    Their admonitions and their tears.

And when death's curtain o'er us falls,
    May heaven dispel the clouds of night,
O ! may we hear the voice that calls:
    "Come, welcome to the realms of light."

THE CREELIN'.

[It was a custom, in certain districts of Scotland, from time immemorial, to "creel" the bridegroom, *i. e.*, to tie a creel upon his back, and to fill it as full of stones as the "heapit measure" would allow, and then to march the young guidman, amidst roars of laughter, before the doors of the clachan. When the bridegroom was beginning to totter beneath the burden, and as the saying is, "upon his last legs," the bride would rush out of the house, and with a gullie knife cut the strings, and make basket and stones play birr upon the ground. This part of the business was usually followed with cheers as loud as the lungs of the on-lookers would permit. I may also add, that no marriage was considered complete till the custom above described had taken place.]

OUR Andrew was a canty lad,
As dink a lad as e'er ye saw,
But now he is baith dowff and sad,
Since Lucy's stown his heart awa'.

On summer nights when dargs were done,
Upon the green he'd dance wi' glee,
But a' the lasses he wad shun,
Though hard they tried to catch his e'e.

But Lucy, she cam' ower the hill,
And Andrew's heart gaed kempin' sair,
For she had cheeks sae rosy red,
And oh ! sae gowden was her hair.

Her e'en did glint sae bonnie blue,
Her neck was like the driven snow,
She had a heart baith kind and true,
As pure as earth can ever know.

He met her in her father's ha',
    He watched the glances o' her e'e,
And aye the mair o' her he saw,
    The mair o' her he wished to see.

And now he gangs just like a ghaist,
    'Mang dowie glens he aften strays;
He derns on the moorland waste,
    And cries on death to end his days.

His coggie clean he canna scart,
    He scunners at his very kail;
At mirkest hour he'll eerie start,
    And wake the echoes wi' his wail.

His hair he never kames ava,
    It's kink'd and matted round his croon,
Belyve, he'll tak' his pipe and blaw,
    And gape and glower up at the moon.

He wears nae ribbon at his knee,
    And when he gangs to kirk or mill,
He looks as sad as sad can be,
    And a' for love o' Lucy Hill.

But Lucy ken'd, in spite o' fate,
    That Andrew lo'ed her unco weel,
Now they are wed, though unco blate—
    She frae his back did cut the creel.

She cut the strings! She whang'd them through!
    And on the ground the creel play'd birr,
Then auld and young cried "Hip-harroo!"
    While some wi' gigglin couldna stir.

Auld Aunty Kirsty beck'd and laugh'd,
    Ye might hae tied her wi' a strae,
Jean Tait, poor woman, lap like daft,
    Syne coup'd, and tumbled down the brae!

A bonnie lass was Jessie Dunn,
She cuist at Jock a 'tatie peelin',
Her very curls danced wi' fun—
As she cried: "Jock, when is your creelin?"

Then Jockie cried: "When ye consent!"
To kiss his Jessie off he ran,
But like a deer awa she went,
Sayin': "Jockie, catch me if ye can."

Now Andrew took his Lucy's hand,
And then they tried to slip away,
But auld John Elder cried out "stand!
For I've a word or twa to say."

John drew a breath, syne said "my lass
Ye're a rail purpose lookin' wife,
I mark'd true smeddum in your face
When ye cam' bleezing wi' the knife.

"I mind fu' weel when I was creel'd,
My wife was just a muleish molly,
She took the dorts, syne roar'd and squeel'd,
And wadna goam the very gully.

"'Afore the doors wi' my big lade
I waggel'd like a willow wand,
Yet still the dour camstery jade,
Wad neither left her fit or hand!

"At length my wind and strength ga'e out
And down I fell wi' sic a ris'le,
Without a shadow o' a doubt
I thought I'd burstit a blood vessel!

"The creel-rope hankit round my throat,
I thought my back had snap'd asunder,
How lang I lay I've e'en forgot,
For that transpired in Eighteen hunder'.

"Tam Blacklock had a bang guidwife,
She cock'd her lug and heard my granes,
She cut the rope and saved my life,
Syne heezed me up frae 'mang the stanes.

"I ga'e a glow'r at Draigle-tail,
Her conduct sairly did deceive me,
That very night she took leg-bail,
Her emigration didna grieve me.

"Now Lucy tak' advice frae me,
Ye'll find it aye the wisest plan,
Until the minit that ye dee
Aye strive to please your ain guidman."

Now Tam Tod said: "John, I've a doubt,
That tongue o' yours wad thole a teather,
See, man! the bride's as white's a cloot
And still ye'll deave her wi' your blether!"

Then Lucy led her Andrew in,
She sneck'd the door wi' tentie care,
She kissed the spot aboon his chin,
Guidsakes! they were a couthie pair.

And thus he spoke: "O! Lucy dear,
I'm glad that creel is aff my back;"
Then Lucy shed a thankfu' tear,
Syne Andrew gave her smack for smack.

Harken, ye wives, 'tween you and me,
In weel waled words I speak ye fair,
Wi' your guidman ne'er disagree,
But strive to ease his load o' care!

Ne'er thraw the mouth, and jeer and jaw,
And stamp your feet an' rair an' shore him,
That is the daftest plan o' a',
Your smiles wad soon "come Paddy o'er him."

And you, ye lasses, loud I pray,
That goodness still may ever guide ye,
Frae good advisement never stray,
And then nae ill can e'er betide ye.

Auld maids! ye're aiblins blest 'bune a',
Your man will never catch a creelin',
The men, ye ken, are just a staw,
They're sae devoid o' sense and feelin'.

And last to a' the human race
(I'm strivin' sair to end this letter),
I fondly trust, wi' help o' grace,
Instead o' worse, we'll aye grow better.

How happy Andrew's wi' his wife,
She lo'es him extraordinar' weel,
She still preserves the gully knife,
But Andrew burnt the muckle creel!

Turning the Key.

THE Shearers had got through the shearin',
The Autumn to an end was wearin';
The kye that browsed 'mang moors and mosses,
Gade hame to sleep in byres and houses.

The sun had set, the stars were blinking,
At his fire-side Tam Swan sat winking,
He ga'e a gaunt, and then quo' he,
"Jenny! Guidwife, gae turn the key,
Right off to bed I e'en maun creep,
For I am fairly daised wi' sleep."
Sae cross the floor auld Tammie shankit,
And soon he crawled aneath the blankit;
The Guidwife scoured baith pat and pan,
Syne cuddled in wi' her Guidman!

A daughter heaven had sent this pair—
A strapping queen, baith fresh and fair,
This bonnie lassie's name was Nell—
Her sweetheart's name was Willy Bell;
The parents left Nell in the nook,
A-glowerin' o'er an auld sang book;
She heard her minnie lock the door—
She heard her father gi'e a snore;
Then frae her seat the lassie loupit,
By some mischance the candle coupit,
She banged it up to blaw it in,
And near-hand burnt her bonnie chin!
She heard the garden-gate play jee,
She made the candle-doup play flee,
Syne slippit aff and turned the key—
Then out she sprang as light's a filly,
To ha'e a courting 'bout wi' Willy.
How heedlessly the moment's fly,
When lovers heave the heartfelt sigh—
They see nae bogles creeping by!
Sleep on the aged couple center'd,
When in the door a Kyloe ventur'd,
It snuffed awhile about the entry,
And syne it edged up to the pantry,
But, finding neither corn nor clover,
The stupid beast began to dover,
Then down it crap upon the floorin'
Near hand where Tammie led the snorin',
'Gainst the bed-post it gave a ristle,
Which soon gar'd Jenny fyke and fistle—
And listen with a tentie ear,
In case auld Satan should appear.
As thus she lay as still's a lammie,
Fast by the side o' sleeping Tammie;
She heard a kind o' unkent breathin'—
Soon terror to her heart was cleavin';
She dunches Tam—she says, "Oh waukin',
Wi' dread my very heart is quakin',

As sure's I live, I hear a snivel
As if it cam' fresh frae the deevil !"
Yet Tammie lay devoid o' thought,
Though fear nailed Jenny to the spot;
At length he muttered "tuts, lie still,
It's naething but our daughter Nell,
Wha's dished wi' sleep and breathing sair,
Or aiblins fashed wi' the night-mare."
He gave a grunt syne round did creep,
Auld Tammie soon was fast asleep.
When winds blaw fair upon life's ocean,
Pride in our hearts aft drowns devotion,
When storms arise we cry to heaven,
And pant and pray to be forgiven !
Now Jenny is my illustration—
Losh ! how she groaned on this occasion !
Her flaff'ring pulse at times stood still,
At times it yerkit like a mill,
Fear fastened on her very eye—
Her every pore weep'd agony !
There is a limit to endurance,
Her inward prayers brought no assurance;
She drew a breath ! She gave a bellow
That woke the very sleeping Kyloe;
Whiff! Tammie out the bed played whack,
And got a-stride the Kyloe's back,
He sat and groaned as if on thorns,
Syne grappled hard a pair o' horns !
The Kyloe sprang—dashed to the door,
The brute re-echoed Tammie's roar.
Fear at ilk hair did rive and rug,
Despair did whistle in his lug,
Sic dismal dread was never ken'd—
His very night-cap stood on end!
As Tammie held by horn and pow
He yelled—"The deevil's got me now !"
While Jenny in her bed did lie
Preparing for eternity!

Out through the yard the beastie loupit,
It funked and plunged and Tammie coupit;
As Nell and Will saw something comin',
Out ower the dyke they baith gade bummin',
Then headlong scoured across the bent,
Their furious shrieks the welkin rent,
For, past the twa the brute gade drivin'—
As if its very hide was rivin',
Poor Willy sair his croon did claw,
While Nelly fairly swoon'd awa!
When time had brought them to their senses,
Hameward they gade wi' few pretenses;
They keekit ower the garden wa',
Hech me! an unco sight they saw,
There Tammie lay besmeared wi' glaur,
And glow'rin' at the evening star!
Nellie instinctive raised his head,
At first, she thought that he was dead,
Yet though his bones were cloured and bloody,
The breath had not gone out his body;
They oxtered him into the hallan,
Then Jenny frae her bed cam' squallin',
Tam eyed her hard, then gave a groan,
Syne whisp'ring speered "If Nick was gone?"
Next morn they to the Priest did trot—
They told him what a gliff they'd got.
The Priest in meditation sicker,
Speered "if the brute did gie a nicker?"
"Na, na," quo' Tam, "it gae a rout;"
The Priest then cried, "I've found it out—
Your deil was nothing but a nowte."
"A nowte?" quo' Tam, "say that again,"
For light cam' into Tammie's brain;
"Ye're right!" he cried, "'tween me and you,
It must hae been our Kyloe-coo."
When Willy spoke a word to Nell,
"I'll take the blame," she cried, "mysel'

For, whan my jo' cam' courtin' me,
I e'en forgot to turn the key."
Quo' Will, "my dear, to end the matter,
The sooner that we're wed the better."
Sweet Nellie blushed and syne consented,
Then hame they a' gade weel contented;
And aye at night, 'tween you and me,
Nell ne'er forgot to turn the key.

A Sabbath Morning in Scotland.

Inscribed to the Rev. John Jennings, D. D., Toronto.

THE morning sun glints up ayont the hill;
The misty clouds of morn have fled away,
Calm is the pool, the sky serene and still,
The lark, exultant, chants his early lay,
The joyful birds sing blythe upon the sprey,
The wings of peace are spread o'er hill and lea,
This is the sacred, holy Sabbath day.
From toil, this morn, the husbandman is free,
From blissful rest he wakes, to bow to God the knee.

His little bairnies start up one by one,
They early learn to know the day of rest;
Wee Maggie asks if frock or bonnet's done?
They clamor to put on their Sunday's best;
The guidwife clasps her infant to her breast,
Warns and commands the noisy to behave;
Wee Will tries on his new-made breeks and vest,
He struts about the wonder o' the lave:
'Gainst pride, the guidman speaks, wi' looks demure and grave.

He fondly takes his Willy by the hand,
And aff they gang to dander round aboot,
To see, perhaps, if dyke or pailing stand,
Or if the wheat or oats begin to shoot;
The kye frae foggage field ha'e broken out,
His collie dog soon answers to his ca';
He pulls a turnip and cuts off the root,
Wee Willy kens the way to wring the shaw,
He sits and glow'rs and eats while daddie mends the flaw.

Adown the bank they ca' the sheep and kye
To where the burnie laves out owre the rocks;
Syne hameward 'cross the bonnie brig o' Dye,
Where weeping willows wave their silv'ry locks.
High on the tree the raven hoarsely croaks,
The lintie sings among the heath'ry braes;
The herds ha'e turned and gathered in their flocks—
Baith hind and herd respect the day o' days—
From lowly shiel and cot ascends the song of praise.

At hame, our guidwife lights the kitchen fire,
And soon the kettle's hissing on the grate,
The cow's been milked and turned frae the byre,
Now milk and porridge fill baith bowl and plate,
The chairs are set—the bairns wi' look sedate,
Afore the porridge cool wad fain begin;
The grace is said—they now nae langer wait;
The guidwife cries, "it is a perfect sin
To see the milk and porridge down Will's apron rin!"

The horn spoons, at length, aside are laid,
Now to the door the bairns fain wad steal,
To gang thereout the boldest is afraid—
Their questions they maun learn and answer weal:
The auld kirk bell sets up a solemn peal,
The cry is heard, "Auld John is at the tow!"
Around the house wi' bairns at her heel—
The guidwife's wits and hands are eident now,
She washes rosy face, and kames the curly pow.

Their bonnie Jessie, unco shy and blate,
Comes ben the house dress'd wi' a braw new goon,
The guidman says, "'twad e'en tak' an estate,
To keep ye a' in meat and claes and shoon."
The guidwife cries, "come hurry, ye'll be late!
Sic moping bairns I'm sure I never saw,
See! there's your pennies for the poor folk's plate"—
The Book o' Books she hands to grit and sma';
Fain is her heart to see them look sae weal and braw.

Now down the garden walk sweet Jessie goes—
She trips sae lightly o'er the grassy knoll,
The scented spearmint pulls and budding rose,
She twines them baith in Willie's button-hole.
The clinking bell at last has ceased to toll,
They hurry aff and gain the kirk-yard road:
See! up the brae yon poor auld bodies toil
Oppressed wi' age and care—a weary load—
And now, baith auld and young have reached the house of God.

Land of my fathers—of the brave and free!
Land where the God of heaven is ador'd!
Land where the patriots humbly bow'd the knee—
Then rose to wave the Standard of the Lord!
My heart, O Scotland! from its inmost chord,
With kindly wishes beats for thee and thine;
O! may thy barns with plenty aye be stor'd,
And freedom's sun forever on thee shine—
Still may your "shield" be Christ, your "buckler" God divine!

TO JAMES MCKAY, ESQ., DETROIT.

Sarnia, Ont., August 18, 1871.

Sir—

THIS evening at the gloamin' grey,
I gat your letter, James McKay,
And glad was I to hear ye say—
And proud to know it,—
That ye're a' in the ordinar' way
About Detroit.

Whan next that ye take up the pen,
There's ae thing I would like to ken,
If ye ha'e won that bonnie hen—
That lassie braw,
To guide the *but* and grace the *ben*
In your bit ha'.

I mind it weel—'fore I was wed,
An unco weary life I led,
Groaning and girning on my bed,
Wi' lonesome moan;
Sae soon's I to the altar sped,
Whiff! Care was gone!

Afore, I'd wander 'bout the braes,
A' nature then seemed sour as slaes,
Then down I'd sit as in a maze,
Aside the burn,
And on the winding waters gaze,
And sigh and mourn!

I'd watch a' nature filled wi' glee—
The lammies sporting on the lea,
The birdies whistling on the tree,
　　Their tender strain;
I didna ken, 'tween you and me,
　　What gar'd me grane!

Ae night I warstled 'mang the ferns,
And tossed amang the whins and birns,
And tald my woes e'en to the sterns,
　　Wi' gruesome croaks,
That scared to death the lang leg'd herons
　　Amang the rocks!

I growled against my low estate,
I envied sair the rich and great,
Till Nature cried: "Man, get a mate,
　　And a bit housie."
Sae faith! ae night I up the gate,
　　And spak' for Lucy!

Hope's tender bud began to grow,
The light o' love began to lowe,
Losh, Jemmy! if ye saw me now
　　Midst bliss supreme!
Stand clear! five bairns I ha'e in tow
　　Upon life's stream.

I'm getting unco auld and stiff,
And glow'ring ower life's dreary cliff;
'Twill no be lang or I play whiff,
　　And close my e'en,
And sail awa in death's dark skiff
　　To the unseen.

Yet still I needna grunt and grane,
I'm no just in the warld alane,
I've wife and bairns to ca' my ain—
　　And when I dee
Nae stranger cauld wi' heart o' stane
　　Will close my e'e!

Now, Jemmy! tak' ye tent, my man,
And try the matrimonial plan;
Remember! life is but a span;
I speak ye fair—
Just buckle hard and fast to Nan
For evermair!

Wi' a' your might tak' my example,
Upon your "whys" and "wherefores" trample,
Just get a wife and raise a sample
O' young McKays;
They'll be, nae doubt, a comfort ample
In your auld days.

Remember me, then, to your Nan,
And kind regards to Bannerman,
And tell the "Major" 'bout the plan
That he maun mak'.
Should death no flash in my bread-pan
I'll soon be back.

THAT'S BUT NAT'RAL.

Inscribed to Duncan Campbell, Esq., a natural born Poet.

"Weel, Jenny," said the Rev. Walter Dunlap to the bride, "do ye like Jock?" "Yes, Sir!" replied Jenny, "I like Jock rale weel." The reverend gentleman smiled in a quiet way, and then said, "that's but nat'ral Jenny, ma woman."

THE spring had brought out the green leaf on the trees,
And the flow'rs were unfalding their sweets to the bees,
When Jock says to Jenny, "come, Jenny, agree,
And just say the bit word that ye'll marry me."
She held down her head like a lily sae meek,
And the blush o' the rose fled away frae her cheek,

And she said, "gang awa, man! your head's in a creel."
She didna let on that she liked him rale weel.
Aye! she liked him rale weel,
O! she liked him rale weel,
But she didna let on that she liked him rale weel.

Now Jock says, "Oh, Jenny, for a twalmonth and mair,
Ye hae kept me just hanging 'tween hope and despair,
But, Oh! Jenny, last night something whisper'd to me—
That I'd better lie down at the dyke side and dee."
To keep Jock in life, she gave in to be tied,
And soon they were book'd, and three times they were cried;
Love danced in Jock's heart, and hope joined the reel;
He was sure that his Jenny did like him rale weel.
Aye! she liked him rale weel,
O! she liked him rale weel,
But she never let on that she liked him rale weel.

When the wedding day cam', to the manse they did stap,
At the door they gat welcome frae Mr. Dunlap,
Wha chained them to love's matrimonial stake;
Syne they a' took a dram and a mouthfu' o' cake,
Then the minister said, "Jock, be kind to your Jenny,
Nae langer she's tied to the string o' her Minnie;
Noo, Jenny, will ye aye be couthie and leal?"
"Yes, Sir," simper'd she, "for I like him rale weel."
Aye! she liked him rale weel,
O! she liked him rale weel;
"That's but nat'ral," he answered, "to like him rale weel."

War and Peace.

When the Lion of England rushed north from his lair,
The welkin re-echoed, "touch me if ye dare!"
Then shoulder to shoulder Scots sprang to the fray
Shouting "Scotland and freedom for ever and aye!"

The tyrant may tremble! the claymores will clash,
And the eye of the clansmen with vengeance will flash—
And the axe of Lochaber its thousands will slay:
Hark! harken, the war-cry "St. Andrew for aye!"

O'er mountain and valley the wild slogans ring,
Up! Rise! draw the sword for our Country and King;
Though blood dye the heather from Tweed to the Spey,
The thistle shall flourish—shall flourish for aye!

Rouse, Scotland! Up Scotsmen! come ruin, come wreck,
No tyrant shall ever put foot on our neck;
Blow trumpet! Sound pibroch the undying lay—
That freedom shall reign in our country for aye!

The beacons are blazing on each mountain crest,
Unquench'd is the fire in each patriot breast;
They fight and they conquer—God is their stay—
Caledonia, their country, for ever and aye!

Be it ever remember'd, the glory and fame
Of Wallace and Bruce, gallant Douglas and Græm,
Of our fathers who fell, but who never gave way—
Their glory was Scotland and freedom for aye!

Now, the sword's in the scabbard—unbuckled's the shield,
The pen is the victor! the Union is sealed—
Ye winds waft the peace-song till time pass away,
And God guard the Thistle of Scotland for aye!

A Kittlin Clatter.

Inscribed to Wm. Barclay, Esq.

YE wee auld fashion'd glow'rin' kittlin,
As sure's I live at mice you're ettlin';
Tuts! in the neuk ye now are settlin'
To tak' a nap,
Ye ha'e win through wi' your bit brattlin'—
Ye're sound's a tap.

Your twa bit e'en are steekit fast,
Unmindfu' o' the wintry blast;
Ye care na' how folk fend or fast—
Midst weal or woe
A sheep's e'e at your tail ye cast
And round ye go!

Guid guide us a'! you're nae-ways lazy,
I ferlie sair ye no grow dizzy;
"Get out my road ye donnert hussy—"
That's Grannie's growl—
"Ye're just amang my feet or claes aye
Ye crawlin' sowl."

"I'll send," quo' she, "I'll send for Jock,
He'll clank ye in an auld mouth pock,
He'll mak ye birr out owre the rock,
Wi' little clatter
Syne ye may splarge an' blaw an' chock
Amang the water."

"Losh! Grannie, let the brute a-be,
We'll strive wi' the bit beast to 'gree,
There's room for it, and you and me—
Rin! Grannie, rin
See there! the aumry door's a-jee;
Great grief! it's in."

Poor brute! ye little ken what's comin',
Dogs will soon at your tail be bummin',
And trees and houses ye'll be climbin'
Wi' fuffs an' granes,
And bairns will at ye hard be slingin'
Baith sticks and stanes.

Now! there ye stand and croon and girn,
Whiff! ye are aff ayont the kirn,
You're out! you're there, baith skin and birn;
What's that i' faith?
Preserve us a'! it's Grannie's pirn—
As sure as death!

There now! ye've cleek'd her auld mutch string,
Down to the floor the mutch ye bring;
Your neck will get an unco wring,
She's hirplin' ben:
I'll save ye yet ye silly thing
Afore she ken.

Here comes my wee bit Nellie toddlin',
An' round about my knee she's hoddlin',
She's now the wee bit pussie coddlin',
In her bit dadle;
She'll no be lang the beastie saddlin',
I'll bet a bodle.

Out loups the cat! down fa's my dautie!
Get out my sight ye nasty catie,
I'll fell ye wi' this muckle tatie;
Come here my hinnie,
Come here, we'll ha'e a couthie chatie,
We'll tell your Minnie.

3

Come to my hand, my wee bit pussie,
Ye aiblins soon will catch a mousie,
An' now, sae lang's I ha'e a housie
    Out owre my head,
Your birses in a plate ye'll souse aye,
    'Mang milk an' bread.

Ye're mair contented than your maister,
Wha still maun pingle, darg, and pester,
Although Dame Fortune aft he's chas'd her,
    Baith e're and late,
The slippery jade, he's ne'er caress'd her—
    E'en to this date!

Soon I maun jouk 'neath death's dark wave,
Soon wintry blasts will owre me rave;
Will ye come mewin' to my grave,
    My wee bit pet?
Or will ye just be like the lave,
    An' soon forget?

YE BALLAD OF JEANIE JOHNSTON.

NOW Tibbie Johnston's daughter
    Gaed doon the burn-brae,
And she sat doon upon the bank,
    Amang the new mawn hay.

'Twas autumn, and the golden sun
    Shone bright o'er hill and dale,
But the cheek o' Jeanie Johnston
    Was unco wan and pale.

The stream o' Watch ran wimplin' clear,
    The lambs danced on the lea,
The lark sang blythesome i' the lift,
    The shillfa on the tree.

The swallow skimm'd the glassy pool,
    The bees humm'd to and fro,
But the heart o' Jeanie Johnston
    Was filled wi' mickle woe.

Now up the haugh there cam' a lad,
    His name was John McBride,
And he sat doon amang the hay
    By Jeanie Johnston's side.

She turned away her head and said,
    "O! gang awa frae me,
For you must know it soon as syne
    Your bride I canna be!"

Now he has said "O! Jeanie dear,
    My love, my joy, my a',
I little dream'd frae your sweet lips
    Such heartless words would fa'!

"Last night, O! Jeanie Johnston,
    Last night, no further gane,
Did ye no vow doon 'mang the birks
    That ye wad be my ain?"

"Last night when I gade hame, John,
    My mother ca'd me ben,
And she did say, 'where ha'e ye been
    I e'en wad like to ken?'

"'This precious moment tell the truth,
    Or dearly ye will rue.'
I hung my head and oh! I said
    That I had been wi' you!

"My mother's face gat red wi' rage,
Her eyes she opened wide,
And then she cried 'ye ne'er shall be
A wife to John McBride!'

"'For I have got for you a man,
His name is John McFee,
And ere a month flies o'er your head
His chosen bride you'll be!'

"She shook her finger and she said,
'Of John McBride beware',
And then my tears cam' rowin' doon,
And Oh! my heart is sair!"

Now John McBride rose to his feet,
An angry lad was he,
And he did swear he'd be the death—
The death o' John McFee!

Then up rose Jeanie Johnston,
And she spoke with a will,
And she did cry "for mercy's sake
His heart's blood do not spill!

"'Tis better far to dree our weird,
And with this plan agree—
That you will wed some other maid,
And I'll wed John McFee!"

He heard her words, he lifeless fell
Down by the water side,
In agony she cried: "I've been
The death of John McBride!"

Now she ran to the running stream,
She ran with rapid pace,
And with her hands the water scoop'd
And laved it on his face.

And soon he open'd up his eyes,
    And when a breath he drew,
She cried "Oh live! Oh! live for me
    And I will live for you!"

The rosy red came to his cheek
    And joy lit up his e'e,
And thus he spoke, "O! Jeanie swear,
    You'll ne'er wed John McFee!"

Then she exclaimed "I here affirm,
    Whatever may betide,
That no man born I'll ever wed
    But thee, my John McBride!"

As thus they stood beside the burn,
    O! what was their dismay,
When Tibbie Johnston like a wraith,
    Cam' bleezing doon the brae.

When she approach'd she cried "woe! woe!
    Oh! what is this I see,
Ye jade! did I not say last night
    Ye must wed John McFee?"

Now John McBride edged cannie up,
    And meek and mim look'd at her;
Then said, "Oh! Tibbie, gi'e consent,
    That I may wed your daughter.

"I ha'e a house and weel filled byre,
    Sax chairs and muckle table,
A pat, a pan, a guid peat-stack,
    A trencher and a ladle!"

Soon Tibbie Johnson ga'e consent,
    Soon to the kirk they ride,
And Jeanie Johnston now is won,
    And wed to John McBride!

When John McFee did hear the news,
He snuffed and gave a sneeze,
Then he lay down upon his back,
And died of heart disease!

Now all ye lovers far and near,
Take warning from this story,
Though sweethearts may say "nay" to-day,
They might say "yes" to-morrow.

SCOTTISH SANGS.

GUIDMAN! losh, I wish ye were through wi' your havers,
About your auld sangs an' your clashes and clavers,
The floor is to scour and the scones are to bake,
The stove is to brush and the carpet to shake;
An' still ye will sit, losh! just hear to the coo,
An' the cacklin' hens and the famishin' soo;
A man sic as you, I'm sure never was born;
Hurry out! or the brutes will be dead ere the morn.

"I've your trousers to mend and your stockin's to dern,
An' ten hanks o' thread to row up on a pirn,
The woo is to card, and the thrums are to reel,
I've the 'taties to wash and the ingans to peel,
The kinlin's to split, and the wood's to be saw'd,
An' water—sax stoups,—frae the well maun be draw'd,
The claes are a' dirty, and as sure as ye're born,
The washin' I canna pit aff till the morn.

"Hech me! can ye no gang an' foother the coo,
And tak out some meat to the hens and the soo;
The beds are to mak' an' the dishes to wash,
An' still 'bout your sangs ye will claver and clash.

Gif ye no gang awa, and look to the horse,
As sure as I live I'll get out a divorce!
Gang awa! I'll come clank owre your head wi' the tangs;
Gif I hear ony mair 'bout your ballads and sangs."

"Guid wife! losh, I hear ilka word that ye say,
But I trow ye maun try to excuse me the day,
Frae Job ye maun strive a bit lesson to learn,
For I'm aff and awa to hear ANGUS FAIRBAIRN."
"Guid man, will ye tak me? losh! ma head's in a creel,
But the coo and the soo may baith roar like the diel,
I'll soon kame ma hair and throw on ma gown,
Ma shawl and ma bonner wi' lace on the croon,
Come, now, let's awa! lock the door—tak the keys"—
And aff the twa gade just as brisk as twa bees,
And, aye they did say, as they hurried alang,
"There's naething sae sweet as an auld Scottish sang."

THE DIALOGUE OF THE BREEKS.

AE morn, as I lay dowie on my back,
Twa pair o' breeks did thus begin to crack :

AULD BREEKS.

"Aye! there ye hing my braw new winsome kimmer,
As proud as ony butterfly in simmer!
Ye look sae trim and trig and unco neat,
I doubt ye'll burst wi' even-doon conceit;
Ye're ironed up, ye shaw nae speck or flaw,
Your coat is glossy and as black's a craw;
O' your brass buttons ye may weel think muckle,
And eke o' that new-fangl'd big horse buckle;
But hooly lad! when ye're as auld as me,
Ye'll no be just sae pleasing to the e'e,

Your steeks will here and there be rippit out,
And baith your knees be plaster'd wi' a cloot;
There is a proverb which I've heard folk say
That aye comes true, "ilk dog will ha'e his day."
The laughing-stock ye'll be baith far and wide,
If ye no strive to burke your pensy pride!
Ye senseless thing! ye needna thraw your mouth,
When ye ha'e tint the spring-tide o' your youth,
Ye'll mind my words, and then my faith will ye
No geck wi' disrespect on sic as me!"

NEW BREEKS.

"Ye antiquated auld mis-shapen rag,
How dare ye open out your blusterin' brag?
Ye're wither'd up just like an autumn docken,
Yet still your havers are a wee provokin';
The like o' you to open up your mouth
And speak to me is impudence forsooth!
Ye're just a thread-bare, worn out worthless carl,
Wi' sic as you I no design to quarrel,
'Twill no be lang I need to thole your clack;
Ye'll soon be rowed and tumbled in a sack—
Sent to the mill wi' some auld raggit body,
And be ripp'd up and workit into shoddy;
Or aiblins yet may hing on broker's pegs,
To be ta'en doon to deck some beggar's legs."

AULD BREEKS.

"Ye brainless birkie, when like me ye're auld,
And a' your steeks are open to the cauld,
Ye'll change your tune—ye'll no sae crousely craw,
For pride like yours I trow will get a fa';
Some cleek or pike may rive ye on the knee,
Or some mischanter hap ye canna see:
Though youth is on your side, yet aft I've seen
The bitter tear row doon frae youthfu' e'en;

This warld's strange, ye dinna ken the snares
That lurk in sofas, stools and sitting chairs;
Sae hold your whisht, although ye're young and stout,
I yet wi' you might see my day aboot."

NEW BREEKS

"Though ye have ae leg hangin' in the grave,
Yet how ye haver, how ye rant and rave!
Since Wilson shaped and clipt me wi' his shears,
My days seem weeks, my weeks appear as years;
Sae I will dance, and crousely I'll be singin',
Sae lang's a button on my waist band's hingin'!
As for the future, I'll no care a flee;
The future no concerns the like o' me!"

AULD BREEKS.

"I was nae worthless guid-for-nothing drab,
When Common clipt me frae a braw new wab,
He stitched me up wi' monie carefu' steeks,
My goodness! then I was a pair o' breeks,
And for a while was like a welcome stranger,
Made muckle o', and lived at heck and manger.
For weeks and months my master took guid care
Frae barkin' dogs and gutters to beware;
And aye at night the stour frae me he whisket.
E're he drew blanket up aboon his brisket;
And when he gaed his winsome lass to see,
She sat sae cosh contented on his knee;
And ance I heard her sae, I do declare,
"That his braw breeks just fitted to a hair."
And weel I mind when on Belle Island's banks,
The twa sat doon to rest awhile their shanks;
The birdies blythesome on the trees were singin',
The bonnie flowers frae monie a stem were hingin',
My master's heart was light, and he did croon
A stave or twa o' some auld Scottish tune;

His sweetheart laughed and said, "to hear your rants
Ye seem uplifted wi' your braw new pants."
My master said, and faith he kissed her mou',
"I'm proud o' them, but far mair proud o' you!"
Now when the twa were yok'd in wedlock's traces,
I was the breeks that hung upon his braces;
And 'fore their first wee bairnie saw the light,
And when our master in the depths o' night
Ran for the howdy—New Breeks, understand
I was the breeks cam' readiest to his hand!
'Gainst wind and water gae my best resistance,
And can look back on a weel spent existence."

NEW BREEKS.

"Tuts! ye auld gomeril, now just haud ye there,
'Bout your auld ways I neither ken nor care;
My master frae his bed will soon be birrlin',
And unco quick he will redd out our quarr'lin',
And sure am I 'twas you that raised the shindie,
And for your pains he'll throw ye out the window."

AULD BREEKS.

"Ye gowk! ye should be wallop'd wi' a rung;
Mair mense and manners then wad rule your tongue!
In bygone days wisdom we learned to prize;
These days seem gone—the bairns are born wise!
The auld and frail are seldom now respected—
They're cuffed aboot, and live and die neglected.
'Gain I had strength I'd gie ye sic a lounder,
As lay ye at my feet as flat's a flounder!"

Now frae his bed the bard did slowly rise,
He gaped awhile, and then he rubbed his eyes,
And thus he spoke: "I've hearken'd your palaver,
Auld Breeks, ye yet stand tapmaist in my favor,
Ye've served me weel—ye've been the wale o' claes,
I'll e'en no cast ye off in your auld days;

When folk grow auld they easy get bamboozil'd,
And tak' a tiff whene'er their temper's tousil'd,
But a kind look or canty word address'd,
Aye cheers their heart and mak's them cock their crest.
And now, New Breeks, I hope ye'll ne'er neglect,
To speak to Aulder Breeks wi' due respect."

MORAL.

Now bairns, tak' tent, be sure ye dinna fail,
To catch the heft and moral o' my tale.
Example take from him who did "engage
To rock the cradle of declining age."

Caledonian Games on Belle Isle.

Inscribed to J. B. Wilson, Esq.

For the better understanding of the following rhyme, it is thought necessary to state that "Hog Island" is situated a short distance up the river from Detroit; that the gentlemen named are respected and prominent members of the Caledonian Club of Detroit; and that they went to the island on a certain day for the purpose of making necessary preparations for the annual games.

THERE was Andrew and Johnnie and Willy,
And Davie—a comical dog—
And a Jedburgh chap they ca' Robin,
Sailed awa' to the Island of Hog.
When into the boat they were sittin',
Quo' Davie, "Bob, feather your oar,"
Syne they dashed and they slashed up the river,
To the tune of "Lochaber no more."
And aye they gaed plowin' and rowin',
Hech! how they gaed sweetin' and reekin',
Awa' to the Island of Hog.

Quo' Johnnie to Willy, "Come, Willy,
Do sing us the 'Wee Pickle Tow,'"
"Just sing it yersel'," answered Willy,
"Or I'll gar ye play bum o'er the bow."
Quo' Robin, "The first man that quarrels,
Wi' this oar I'll play crack on his croon,
Sae steek up your lip, neighbor Willy,
And Johnnie, ye Kirk Yetholm loon."
And aye they gaed jawin' and blawin',
Losh! how they gaed barkin' and bitin'
Awa' to the Island of Hog.

When on to the island they jumpit,
The boat to a tree they did tie,
Quo' Davie, "I'd herrin' for supper,
This mornin' I feel unco dry."
He claw'd at his head like a harrow,
Then out from his pouches did draw
A bottle o' Hielan' Glendronach,
And a mutchkin o' real usqueba.
And syne they sat girnin' and laughin',
Gosh! how they sat puffin' and smokin',
Awa' on the Island of Hog!

And when they a' got a bit toothfu',
And when the drink got to their wames,
Quo' Andrew, "Come, freens, let us dander,
And look at the grund for the games."
Then awa through the woods they gaed laughin',
And when they got up to the place,
Quo' Robin to Willy, "Come, Willy,
Losh, man, I will try ye a race."
And soon they gaed sprachlin' and rinnin',
Wow! how they gaed pechin' an' bleezin'
Awa' on the Island of Hog!

"I'll race ye and beat ye," quo' Willy,
Then awa' o'er the green they did loup,

But Willy played clank on his stomach,
And Robin fell down on his doup,
Then they leugh till their sides were near burstin'.
Quo' Robin, "My nose I ha'e bled;"
Quo' Johnnie, "Come, Robin, get up, man,
Did ye think ye was gaein to bed?"
And sair they gaed whummlin' and tumblin',
Bang! how they went clitin' and scraughin',
Awa' on the Island of Hog!

And now they began to the wrestlin',
Sair, hard were their tussles and rugs,
At the links o' the neck and the brisket,
At shoulder-blades, haffits and lugs.
How teughly they stuck to the business,
For the feck o' a couple o' hours,
Till their claes just in ribbons were hangin',
And their banes were a covered wi' clours.
And aye they gaed gripin' and ripin',
Haith! how they gaed skitin' and slippin',
Awa' on the Island of Hog!

By this they were a' gettin' roupit,
Wi' a drappie their gizzards did slake,
Then Dave round his head swung the hammer—
Wi' a bang baith gaed clash in the lake!
Then Andrew began to the puttin',
Slick! the stane to his shouther did raise,
But it slippit somehow frae his clutches,
And cam' yerk on the end o' his taes!
And aye they gaed dreepin' and creepin',
Wow! how they gaed dragglin' and limpin',
Awa' on the Island of Hog!

And syne they began to the jumpin',
Dave lap like a hen aff her eggs;
Then Andrew cried, "Johnnie, look at me,"
Ga'e a spring and maist broke baith his legs.

And next they began to play quoits,
Jock's quoit gaed clean aff the track,
It gaed up in the air like a feather,
Then cam' down upon Jedburgh's back.
And still they went flingin' and ringin'
My! how they gaed backin' and whackin',
Awa' on the Island of Hog!

On receipt o' the knock Robin loupit,
Syne roared like a mad parish bull,
"Haud your tongue, man; keep still, man," quo' Davie,
"And be thankfu' it's no' split your skull."
Quo, Andrew, "I think we'll be gaein',
Wi' terror my very heart's filled;
If we stay ony langer I'm fearin'
Ilka soul o' us a' will be killed."
And oh! they stood whingin' and gruin',
Man! how they stood glaikin' and glunchin',
Awa' on the Island of Hog!

"Losh! Andrew, ye're right, man," quo' Davie;
"My very heart's blood's on the shiver,
For somehow I canna help thinkin'
We're sure to be drowned in the river;"
Yet ilka ane swore to the ither,
Afore they gaed aff to their hames,
That they'd try hard and sair to do better
At the Grand Caledonian Games.
Then hame they cam' thuddin' and scuddin',
Hech! how they cam' swearin' and tearin',
Awa' frae the Island of Hog!

A PASTORAL.

WRITTEN ON THE OCCASION OF JAMES FORSYTH, ESQ., LEAVING DETROIT, FEBRUARY 1ST, 1871.

ARCHY—"Come, Willy man, come in and sup some
drammack,
And tell us a' the news aboot Hamtramack;
Has your guidwife gat hale and weel and canty?
Does still the ague hing aboot your Aunty?
Has Jean Galbraith gat buckled to Tam Cleaver?
I hope the bairns ha'e no the scarlet fever!
Ye look sae dowff, sae dowie and downcast,
Ye look like ane that hasna' broke his fast,
Ye look like ane dumfounder'd wi' despair!
Come man, sit down and tell us a' your care."

WILLY—"I weel I wat, I do feel unco wae!
A lade o' grief hangs owre me night and day—
The smell o' parritch fairly maks me scunner,
An' the guid wife, as sure as death I shun her;
Whan e'en the bairns come climbin' on my knee,
I cry 'get aff! for guid sake let me be.'
The guidwife tries her best to ease me care—
Nae words can calm the bosom o' despair;
Aside the fire I sit and sigh and grane,
Though weel I ken my grief is a' in vain.
At times I tak' a dänder doon the yard,
For the bit flowers I've now lost a' regard;
Last week I had some apple shoots to graft—
As sure's I live I think I'm gaein daft—
I took the shoots and midst my granes and grunts,
I e'en did graft them on some auld kail runts!
Where bonnie flowers did spring the weeds now grow;
I see the weeds—I stand and claw my pow;

I canna use the spade to delve or dig—
My pruning knife ne'er sneds the useless twig;
The watering pan beneath the willows lie—
The flowers hang down their heads and fade and die;
The sangs o' birds did ance my bosom cheer,
Their notes now fa' in discord on my ear."

ARCHY—"For mercy's sake what's wrang—ha'e ye the ague?
Or worse than that, ha'e ye gat the lumbago?"

WILLY—"O! Archy man! I'm unco laith to say,
Our bosom friend—our Jamie's gaun away.
I've kent him lang—he aye was true as steel;
There's nane can ken the bitter grief I feel;
There's few can ken how ill it is to part
Frae him we love—the brother o' our heart."

ARCHY—"Preserve us a'! is Jamie gaun to leave?
There's mair than you wi' bitter grief will grieve;
He aye was kind—sae gentle and sae mild—
An honest man—a sage—at heart a child,
No words were his of selfishness or cant;
His purse was open to his friends in want;
If want or woe his fellow mortal griev'd,
His heart responded and his hand reliev'd.
In learning, we maun own he is our daddie,
He's just a kind o' walkin' Cyclopædia;
He's read the works o' Reid and famous Locke,
He kens the law frae Lyttleton and Coke;
Can gie ye screeds frae Burns and Scott and Brown,
And Rhymer Tam wha lived in Ercildown;
He glories in the fame, the works and style
O' that great thinker they ca' Tam Carlyle.
I weel I wat his life has no been idle,
But best o' a' he ne'er forgot his Bible.
O! doleful hour! O melancholy day,
We'll hae nae joy when Jamie gangs away!"

WILLY—"Where'er he gangs, I'm sure I wish him weel,
'Midst a' his care, he was a canty chiel'.
His head is crammed wi' wisdom and wi' lair,
He rose victorious o'er the word 'despair.'
When he's awa, where'er his lot be cast,
I fondly trust his cares will a' blaw past.
May health and plenty cheer his ain fireside—
His wife and son, his comfort and his pride;
'Mang men o' worth, in the first rank we class him—
Where'er he bides, may God forever bless him."

ARCHY—"Thae's bonnie words, I'm sure ye speak them
true.
Will ye no tak a dram to weet your mou?
The back unto the burden we maun bend,
'And mak the best o' what we canna mend.'"

LAMENTATION FOR MIKE GILL.

A CELEBRATED PLAYER ON THE UNION PIPES.

Respectfully inscribed to the Hon. Wm. Adair.

DETROIT folks are drown'd in woe,
Down o'er their cheeks the salt tears flow,
Death e'en has dealt an unco blow,
And frae us ta'en
A man who never had a foe—
Mike Gill is gane.

We kent poor Mike for monie a year—
His sterling worth demands a tear,
Upon this earth he had nae peer—
He stood alane;
We weel may wail beside the bier
O' him that's gane!

When nights got lang, and folk got douce,
When Mike cam' in, we soon got crouse,
Baith glee and gladness were let loose—
We were sae fain;
But grief now reigns in every house
Since Mike is gane!

The auld folk liked him unco weel,
The young folk followed at his heel,
The lasses aften filled his creel
Wi' beef and bane;
But now he's gat his hinmost meal—
Alas! he's gane!

When marching 'neath the Stars and Stripes,
'Twas grand to hear him blaw the pipes;
Now printers, sobbing, set the types,
Wi' grief and pain;
Het, waesome tears the Bard now wipes
For him that's gane!

We weel may sit about the burn,
And in dark glens and valleys mourn,
And ilka kind o' comfort scorn,
Wi' goustie mane;
Alas! alas! he'll ne'er return—
He's ever gane!

His pipes ha'e gien their lang, last hum,
Again we'll never hear them bum,
They're hanging now ayont the lum
On their bit chain;
Their breath has fled, alas! they're dumb—
Like him wha's gane!

For guidsake ne'er let Barclay know
That Mike lies cauld and stiff below,
Poor man! he'd ne'er get o'er the blow—
He'd break life's chain,
Or, chew for aye the cud o' woe
For him that's gane!

When Mike play'd up an Irish reel,
We neither minded maut or meal,
But up and down, and round we'd wheel,
And plunge and strain;
Now in the ranks o' grief we squeel
Since he is gane!

When Johnston frae toon lots would part,
He aye set Mike up in a cart,
'Twas then we heard the minstrel's art
And canty strain;
He'll ne'er blaw mair at wake or mart—
Alack! he's gane.

He ne'er was known to hum and look
And glow'r upon a music-book,
But just sit smiling in the nook,
And drink a drain;
Ae finger had the crotchet crook
On him that's gane.

When he was cuffed about wi' care,
He took a dram and whiles took mair,
But never fell frae aff a chair
Wi' drunken grane;
Now frae the roots we rive our hair—
Woe's me! he's gane.

Ae night he cam' fu' crouse and trig,
To play us up a blythesome jig,
But oh! he gat an unco dig—
It soon was plain
That he had crossed death's dismal brig—
He's gane! he's gane!

The doctors round about him press'd,
They laid their ear upon his chest,
They placed their fingers on his wrist,
And jug'lar vein:
But Mike did never cock his crest,
For he was gane!

Down wheie the weeping willows wave
James Sutherland has filled Mike's grave,
And at his feet has set a stave,
At's head a stane,
Which tells McGraw and a' the lave
That Mike is gane!

We trace Mike's faults to Adam's fa'—
Mike had some faults, but they were sma'—
His virtues overtopped them a',
I here maintain,
And hope the UNION PIPES he'll blaw,
Where'er he's gane!

FOLK SHOULD AYE BE EQUAL YOKIT.

Inscribed to C. Taylor, Esq. Sarnia, Ont.

AULD Scotland! loud I sing your praise,
Your honest men and wives sae gawsie,
May they aye walk in wisdom's ways,
And keep the cantle o' the causey!

May peace and plenty be their lot—
Contented wi' guid brose and parritch,
And still on Sundays boil the pot,
And ne'er forget their single carritch!

Auld Scotland, ye're a stalwart chield!
The Southern foe could never whang ye,
Faith! set ye on the fighting field,
The very deevil couldna bang ye!

May a' your bairns be aye discreet,
  Ha'e a clean sark and Sunday jackit,
Sair! sair, the bard wad roar and greet
  Should Scotia's bairns be disrespekit!

Her bonnie lasses! guid keep me,
  They've led me monie a weary brattle,
Scouring at night o'er moor and lea,
  And swarfing sair the out-door cattle.

Ae back-end night, O! hech how me,
  I gat a mair than ordinar' fright;
Until the very day I dee,
  I'll ne'er forget that unco night.

On the har'st-rig I shore wi' ane—
  Her maiden name was Nellie Martin;
Love, feverish love, on me struck in,
  And Nell and I began the courtin'.

She had a waist sae jimp and sma',
  And when she smiled she looked sae bonnie,
And then her lips, preserve as a'—
  They were as sweet as heather honey!

How grand! how lovely was her face,
  A perfect heaven was in her e'e!
To crown her charms she had a grace
  That played the deil wi' mair than me!

'Twas aughteen years, no ae day mair,
  Since first she gave her infant cry—
She cam' just at the Lammas fair,
  As Session Records testify.

She lived sax miles out ower the bent,
  At a bit house ayont the glen;
Ae night I couldna stay content,
  I fain wad see my bonnie hen!

I sleely stole aff like a mouse,
And o'er the moor I soon gaed scrievin';
The clouds by this had broken loose—
The winds blew out the lights o' heaven!

I gropit o'er the auld wood brig,
Got through the birks and past the rashes;
Without a'e lee, whan at Whinrig,
Losh! I began to ban the lasses!

The lightnings leaped across the sky,
I lap out o'er stone dykes and fences;
I thought I heard the kelpies cry—
"That gouk has surely tint his senses."

At times I swat wi' downright dread,
And ance I foundered 'mang the glaur;
As forth I gade wi' swirlin' speed
I headlang plunged out o'er a scaur!

Hech me! thought I, I'm done for noo,
My heart-strings gae an unco pull,
Fear jumpit down my very mou,
Syne struck the keybone o' my skull!

I hae had monie an unco fright,
But a' the frights that e'er I got
Are nothing to that desperate night,
As down that fearfu' gulph I shot!

Oh! Nellie, in my hours of ease
I've worshiped e'en your very locks,
I little dreamed through space I'd bleeze,
And kill mysel' 'mang stanes and rocks!

I thought on Nellie's lock o' hair,
That o'er my throbbing bosom hung,
I tried to roar, but in the air
Fear shut the hinges o' my tongue!

As down and down and down I fell,
    A pleasing notion filled my head,
Wi' my last breath to cry on Nell,
    Syne close my eyes amang the dead.

An unco job I had to land,
    Mang whins, and sheep, and muckle stanes,
Dumfounder'd! I cam' to a stand
    That jumbled up my very brains.

That night I could not see my Nell—
    For broken collar banes and legs;
At length I gave a dismal yell
    That echoed 'mang the hills and craigs!

The coward sheep scoured to the hills,
    The foxes to their holes ran rife,
The cattle turned up their tails
    And fled as if for very life!

The corbies croaked out o'er my head,
    Nae doubt expecting my last groan,
And other brutes famed for their greed,
    Cam' out to see what was gaun on.

And there I lay, and girned and grat,
    With agony my thoughts ran wild,
Aye! there I lay, I weel I wat,
    As helpless as a little child.

Next morn, the wind had blawn its warst,
    When Tam-the-herd cam' to me hotchin',
He leugh till he was like to burst—
    Syne speered "gif I was at the poachin'."

"Na! na!" quo' I, "Tam get a cart—
    For ance ye're fairly aff your eggs;
I doubt I've broken Nellie's heart,
    Forby ma collar banes, and legs."

Tam ran to get a horse and cart,
I thought 'mang men he was the marrow;
A clud o' grief cam' ower my heart,
As back he dash'd wi' a wheelbarrow.

He trailed me in, he wheeled and wheel'd,
Ungratefu' like I did abhor him;
Though Tam was a lang winded chield,
For ance he had his wark afore him.

He pushed and wheeled and better wheel'd,
At ilka jolt my banes did harrow,
Twice o'er he stagger'd—thrice he reel'd,
And sent me headlang out the barrow!

We laired and founder'd in a bog,
And oh! an unco job had Tam,
He swore against his collie dog,
And ance he prayed and sung a psalm.

Wi' sair ado he gat me hame
He wheeled me up to the bed-stok,
Quo' he, "I am baith tired and lame,
Wi' hurling you since four o'clock!

"Gif e'er ye gang that gate again,
May I be whipit, hanged or shot,
By day or night, in wind or rain,
Ye'll lie for me until ye rot."

My grannie cried wi' accents wild,
"What's that ye've brought wi' sic a hurl?"
Quo' Tam, "it is your ain grandchild
I'm posting to the other warl'."

Nine weeks I lay upon my bed,
Death like a herd did on me whistle;
And in that time my Nell got wed
To an auld sumph ca'd Patie Russell!

Ah! Nell, ah! Nell, ye ne'er can ken
  What I for you ha'e had to suffer,
But warst o' a' to caickle ben—
  Wi' that auld groaning, girning buffer.

And yet, I still may crously cra',
  That I fell through frae Nellie's chains;
She drives Pate's head against the wa',
  And kicks and scarts his very banes.

Ae day she coursed him like a hare,
  She ran him round and round the stable,
She just had breath and naething mair
  To knock him senseless wi' the paidle!

'Twas a' Pate's blame, the donnert fool,
  I wadna greet though he was chockit,
I'm sure he might ha'e learned at school—
  That folk should aye be equal yokit.

ROB TROTTER'S GIMMER.

THE snaw lay braid-cast on the grund,
  I guess twal inches deep,
When Robbie Trotter frae the hill
  Drove doon a flock o' sheep.
As he cam' past Killpallet burn,
  The sky began a scowlin',
The feath'ry snaw began to fa',
  The angry winds gaed howlin'.

He had twa dogs, ane took the pet,
  And 'gan to whinge and whimple;
Rob raised his cleek wi' a' his might
  And struck it on the rumple!

It ga'e a howl, sprang in the air,
  Then fell back fair confounded,
It clapped its tail atween its legs,
  And ower the dyke it bounded!

Rob whistled on it loud and lang,
  And raised an unco racket,
Then said, "the blasted brute's gane hame,
  I hope the deil may tak' it."
'Mang blinding drift Rob did his best
  To keep his sheep in order,
As he was bound by hook or crook
  To take them ower the border.

Some o' the drove were yald and strong,
  And some were waff and worn out,
And these, at times, frae holes and bogs
  He pulled by tail and horn out.
When he gat to the Rinklaw-hill,
  He felt bumbazed and worret,
And trowed that to his journey's end
  He never would win forrit.

He glower'd whiles at his finger ends,
  To see if they were frozen,
And whiles he'd raise his hand to feel
  If still remained his nose on.
He thought upon the lass he lo'ed,
  Her face, her shape and carriage,
Prospective bliss cheered up his heart,
  And freshen'd up his courage.

The silv'ry moon frae 'mang the cluds
  Now got a kind o' clearance,
Rob's heart grew light and then he said—
  "There's nought like perseverance."
Now when he gained the plantin' side,
  And cleared the Muirtoon entries,
He smak'd his lips and thought 'bout bread,
  And yill fresh frae the gauntrees.

Now at the turnin' o' the road
    There stood a house and stable;
The drifted snaw lay hard and fast
    Up to the very gable.
The yauldest gimmers ga'e a spring,
    And left the waff ahint,
And climbed the riggin' o' the house,
    Afore Rob Trotter kent.

He glower'd right up! wi' a' his heart
    He stood and cursed their folly;
Then after them like fire he flew,
    Fast followed by his collie.
Within the house wee Tailor Will
    Was thrang at his devotions,
He lent his ear, and lo! he heard
    Unearthly strange commotions.

The blaain' o' the jumpin' sheep
    Did gar him stare wi' wonder,
And when he heard Rob Trotter roar,
    His pulse struck 'yont the hunder.
He grasped his Peggy by the hand,
    Laigh on his hunkers bended,
Then yelled, "my day of grace is gone,
    My pilgrimage is ended!"

A lump o' soot fell doon the lum,
    And struck him on the ear,
He keekit round, then cried, "by jing!
    Auld Nick will soon be here!"
He sprang wi' dread across the floor,
    Syne crawled aneath the table;
While to the aumry Peggy flew,
    And seized the 'tatie ladle!

She swung it round and round her head,
    Then yelled, "Auld Nick! by jimney,
Ye'd better gang the road ye cam',
    And no come doon our chimney!"

Rob, half in wrath and half in fun,
  Cried, "haud your tongue, ye limmer,"
Without ae thought, right doon the lum
  He flang a black-faced gimmer!

Will jumpit frae his hiding hole,
  Yet, 'fore his bed he wan till,
Gosh! Peggy raised her instrument,
  And felled it on the cantle!
When William heard the death blow gi'en,
  He took a dwamish tremor,
He skellied round, then roared, "losh! Peg,
  It's unco like a gimmer!"

Peg headlang ran across the floor,
  Then fell out ower the cradle,
And as she couped, she screamed, "Oh! Will,
  I've broke my 'tatie ladle!"
Will heezed her up, Rob op'd the door
  And hurried up the entry,
He viewed the scene, then laughed and said,
  "That sheep stow in your pantry."

The guidwife soon got o'er her swarf—
  Spoke to Rob Trotter ceevil,
While Will remarked, "as sure as death
  I thought it was the deevil!"
He shook his fist at the dead sheep,
  Then said, "lie still, my hearty,"
And then he turned to Peg and said,
  "Next week we'll ha'e a party!"

The Wallace Monument.

Inscribed to James Black, Esq.

STAND ever! freedom's monument,
Where freedom had its birth,
In honor of the bravest knight
That ever breathed on earth!

In memory of great Wallace Wight,
Whose daring, dauntless heart
Did never crouch to foreign foe,
Or Scotland's cause desert.

When cold and chill was freedom's hand,
And faint and fainter grew
Her fluttering breath, great Wallace rose,
And loud her trumpet blew!

The eagle from the rocky cliff
Soared proudly to the sky;
Watching its flight—"Soldiers!" he cried,
"Freedom can never die!"

The droukit thistle raised its head
That erst hung pensylie,
As if it knew the deathless creed—
"Who dares to meddle me?"

The Warrior cried "on to the front,
On, soldiers, to the field,
To fight for God and liberty,
To die but never yield!"

Stand ever, freedom's monument,
Where freedom had its birth,
In honor of the bravest knight
That ever breath'd on earth!

To A. H. Wingfield, Esq.,

Author of the beautiful ballad, "There's Crape on the Door."

WINGFIELD, I'm glad to hear ye still
Are climbing up Parnassus hill;
Losh, man! the words ye clink wi' skill—
How sweet they fa',
Take my advice, ne'er quit the quill,
But screed awa.

Though gowks may jeer, and gomerils ban,
Sing up! sing blythe! my bonnie man,
And do the best that e'er ye can—
Ne'er mind their say,
Rejoice! that genius guides your han',
And tunes the lay.

When I to rhyming did begin,
The fient a hair I'd on my chin;
And when I show'd my critic kin
The hame-spun waft,
They'd say, "just drown him in the linn,
He's clean gane daft."

They'd laugh and smirk at my pretense,
And say "the rhyme was void o' sense,
'Twas wrong in grammar, mood and tense,—
I was a fool."
They'd cry, "your harp hang on a fence,
And gang to schule."

Wi' ilka word they had some fau't—
That line was stolen from Pope or Watt,
That sentance was frae Thompson gat,
That ane frae Hogg;
They'd ca' me a cat-witted brat,
And thievish rogue.

I'd bite my nails, and burn and blush,
My heart's blood through my veins would rush,
I couldna stand it—like a cush
I would retreat,
Syne, down ayont a dyke or bush,
I'd sit and greet.

In winter when the curlew flies,
And tempests hurl athwart the skies,
I'd listen to earth's sounds and sighs,
And nature's croon,
O'er earthly clouds my soul would rise,
To heaven abune!

When floods cam' gushing down the hill,
And swelling wide the wee bit rill,
As sure as death—I mind it still—
In some lone nook,
I'd stand and learn poetic skill
Frae nature's book.

A snow-drop on its bielded bed
Would raise its modest virgin head,
My very heart to it was wed
With nature's chain;
And tears o' joy would o'er it shed,
I was sae fain!

And when the bonnie spring would come,
When bees around the flowers would bum,
And linties were nae langer dumb
The woods amang,
'Twas there wi' them I learned to hum
My wee bit sang.

Beyond the birks where cowslips grow,
And violets spring upon the knowe,
The Muses decked my youthfu' brow
Wi' roses fair,
And bending low I breathed a vow,
Their joys to share.

Then in the gladsome summer days
I'd wander 'mang the heath'ry braes,
And hear the lark sing nature's praise
Far up the sky:
On fancy's wing my soul would gaze
On heaven high!

Nature would guide my careless feet
To where the blackbirds sang sae sweet;
For hours my heart with joy would beat
To list their lay,
Unmindful that the stars did greet
The gloamin' grey.

When darkness wrapt the mountain's head,
And gloom o'er glen and valley spread,
Then o'er me came an eerie dread—
A nameless fear,
A soul-commingling with the dead—
A heaven near!

Wingfield! my summer tide's awa,
My autumn leaf begins to fa',
And vulture death begins to gnaw
And hover near,
Yet still I'll rant and rhyme for a'
Sae lang's I'm here.

I hae nae wish to gather gear,
My muse is a' my comfort here,
My Pegasus is horse and meer,
That heaven has sent,
And while the beastie I can steer,
I'll be content.

Though grief has racked you to the core,
Take up your harp—sing as in yore;
Ye still hae monie joys in store—
I hope and pray
That crape may ne'er hang on your door
For monie a day!

HOHENWINDSOR.

Inscribed to James Fraser, Esq.

IN Windsor when the moon was high,
When every throat was parched and dry,
There rose to heaven a fearful cry—
Of wild despair and agony.

For Windsor saw a dreadful sight,
A thunderbolt at dead of night
Did smash the Windsor pump outright,
And knocked it to eternity.

Then rushed the matron and the maid,
Then Fraser drew his battle blade,
And Bartlett cried, "Go find a spade
And dig my grave immediately."

Then Cameron raised a fearful wail,
That shook the very Sandwich jail,
When Black put on his coat of mail
To fight with him most furiously!

The combat deepens! blood and blows!
The claret flies from every nose,
Far redder than the reddest rose
That blooms in Dougall's nursery!

Few, few of them will see the morn,
Far better had they ne'er been born,
The scythe of death reaps them like corn,
And grinds them in his granary!

Weep, sun, in your triumphal car,
May sackcloth hang from every star,
May earthquakes rend the earth ajar,
And mountains leap distractedly.

The streets of Windsor reek with gore,
The pump, alas ! has gone before ;
Hang dismal grape on every door—
And die in great perplexity !

THE SCOTT CENTENARY.

Read at the Banquet, Russell House, Detroit, August 15, 1871.

HUNDRED years have rolled away,
This morn brought in the natal day
Of one whose name shall live for aye.

Beside the clear and winding Forth
Was born the "Wizard of the North ;"
The Muses circled round his bed,
And placed their mark upon his head ;
And nature sang a grand refrain
As Genius claimed his wondrous brain,
For every bird in bush or brake,
Beside the silv'ry stream or lake,
Sang blythly on their leafy throne,
In honor of the "Great Unknown !

The Thistle raised its drooping head :
The lark forsook his heather bed,
Shook from his wing the dew drop, moist,
And on the golden cloud rejoic'd ;

The classic Tweed took up the lay,
The Yarrow sang by bank and brae,
And Ettrick danc'd upon her way.
The daisies by the crystal wells
Smiled sweetly to the heather bells;
And rugged craig and mountain dun
Exulted he was Scotia's son!

Time sped, and from that brilliant brain
There issued many a martial strain;
He sang of knight and baron bold,
Of king and clown in days of old—
Though dead and gone, and passed away—
Forgotten in the mould'ring clay,—
We read, we trow, his magic brain
Brings back the dead to life again!
He sang of men who ne'er would yield
In border fray or battle field.
Yes! on the page of endless fame
He wrote of many a deed and name;
How patriot heroes dared to die
For God, for right and liberty!

We see the beacon on the hill,
The slumb'ring earth no more is still,
For borne upon the midnight gale
The slogan's heard o'er hill and dale,
The din of battle and the cry
That echoed through the vaulted sky,
As warriors fell, and rose and reel'd,
And died on Flodden's fatal field!

The minstrel loved auld Scotland's hills,
Her gow'ny braes and wimpling rills,
He loved the land that gave him birth—
A land beloved o'er all the earth;

There stood the brave in weal or woe,
Who never crouched to foreign foe—
Who stood in battle like a rock,
And snapped in twain the tyrant's yoke!

O! Scotland, thou art dear to me!
Thou land of song and chivalry!
There Scott and Burns, and many more,
Did pencil nature to the core—
There Wallace held the foe in scorn,
And Scotland lives in Bannockburn!
And every patriot, far or near,
In foreign land, or Scotia dear,
In castle proud, or lowly cot,
Reveres the name of WALTER SCOTT!

A PRECIOUS JEWEL.

Inscribed to W. Wanless, Esq., Sarnia, Ont.

WOA, Pegasus! stand still, ye rip,
Stand still, ye supple, skitin' sorra,
Woa, stand, or I the thread tak' up—
The very first thread o' my story.

A lassie lived wast at Mayshiel,
And wow, but she was fair and friskie,
I here confess, I lo'd her weel,
Though she play'd me an unco pliskie.

We had been bairnies at the schule;
Somehow we aye crap close thegether;
We learned our lessons on ae stool—
Where ane was, faith, ye'd find the other!

Whan schule was out we'd rin and play,
And gowans pu' sae blythe and cheerie :
Wi' lightsome step I'd climb the brae,
And cull the rowans for my dearie.

At the brae-fit, she'd stand and watch,
Her e'en wad glint wi' sweet emotion,
As nuts or rowans she wad catch,
While doon I'd look wi' pure devotion!

Twice twenty years since that ha'e gane;
Though to the verge o' life I'm tap'rin',
Yet still I see her smile fu' fain,
And kep the rowans in her apron!

I yet can see her dimpled cheek,
Her bonnie curls waving free,
Aft in my dreams I hear her speak,
And see her laugh wi' pawkie glee!

How aft we'd sit doon i' the dell,
And twine and shape the rushes green,
My rushy-cap, I needna tell,
Was fashion'd aye for bonnie Jean.

In har'st, we laid aside our book,
And 'hint the shearers we wad pingle,
To Jeanie, in ayont the stook,
I'd sleely hand my wee bit single.

I'd tak' her hand when nae ane saw,
Then she wad blush an' look amiss;
Her lips I durst nae pree ava—
The very thought was perfect bliss!

We lo'ed wi' perfect love divine—
Nature designed us for ilk other;
I'm sure this day she wad be mine,
If death had ca'd away her mother.

For monie a year I courted Jean,
 And aft she vow'd to be my ain;
The weddin'-day was set I ween,
 When faith, her love began to wane.

Ae night her faither look'd sae sour,
 Her mother skellied wi' a'e e'e,
And syne she said: "Tam, ye are poor,
 Ye'd better let our Jean a-be."

Quo I, "Guidwife," as up I rose,
 "I lo'e your daughter true as steel."
But faith, she turned up her nose,
 And faith, I turned upon my heel.

When at the door I ga'e a keek,
 A waesome keek out o'er my shouther,
I saw a tear on Jeanie's cheek,
 And ower my cheek there ran another.

My Jean I never saw nae mair—
 She slighted me for lack o' siller;
In twa short weeks I do declare,
 My lass got buckled to the Miller.

For monie a weary night and day
 I groaned and yattered 'gainst my fate,
But now, at length, I'm glad to say,
 I'm somewhat better at this date.

Now ilka lad tak' my advice—
 Whene'er your lass gets out o' tune,
Just let her gang—though e'er sae nice,
 Aye strive to keep your heart abune.

Be like the man that had a kist,
 And when he loosen'd aff the rope
He raised the lid—his all he missed,
 But found the precious jewel—HOPE!

Too Much Liberty.

Inscribed to James Anderson, Esq.

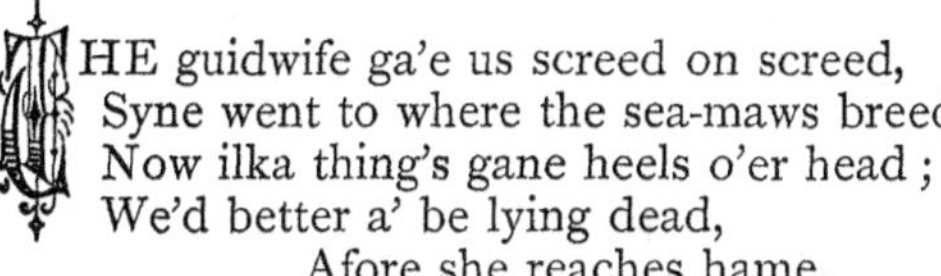

HE guidwife ga'e us screed on screed,
Syne went to where the sea-maws breed,
Now ilka thing's gane heels o'er head;
We'd better a' be lying dead,
Afore she reaches hame.

The sow runs squeelin' round the yard,
The dog has e'en lost a' regard;
Our Jean sits bletherin' wi' the Laird,
And gecks at his lang tousie beard,
Her mither's no at hame.

Whene'er the maut got 'bune the meal,
The sight o' her wad gar us squeel,
Like rattans into holes we'd steal,
Guid faith! we'd sooner face the de'il—
Than her wha's comin' hame.

There's nane now scarts the parritch pat,
The soot has got among the saut,
The Laird has drank up a' the maut,
The Doctor is as blind's a bat—
The guidwife's no at hame.

We'll a' be forced to join the total,
The cork will soon be in the bottle,
The press-key placed in the kist shottle;
We'll ha'e to smoke fear's very dottle—
When our guidwife comes hame.

The soap lies soakin' in the plate,
We've hounded care out at the gate,
We've lost the very day and date,
We tumble headlang aff the sate,
When our guidwife's frae hame.

At night, like owls, the lasses whup,
Next morn ye canna rouse them up;
They've broken ashet, plate and cup,
We'll soon ha'e neither bite or sup;
At times we wish her hame.

Our Jocks, our Peters and our Wills,
Just a' gang roaring round like bulls,
And kicking chairs out o'er the stools,
And cracking ane another's skulls,
When our guidwife's frae hame.

Wee Tam sits glunching in the nook,
With face and hands as black's the crook,
He glooms e'en at the Bible-book,
And on his lessons winna look,
When the guidwife's frae hame.

When once her foot's o'er the door stane,
A' our excuses will be vain,
Though tears come dashing down like rain,
Her antidote will find the bane—
See there! she's coming hame.

She's hame, and she has felled the soo,
She's flung the dog out o'er the coo,
She's mauled us till we're black and blue—
Transgression's bitter cud we chew
Since our guidwife cam' hame.

She's bearded discord in its lair,
The Laird and Jean kicked down the stair,
Now Justice sits high on his chair,
And Virtue cries to Vice "beware!"
Our guidwife's now at hame.

MORAL.

The knave 'bout liberty may shout,
The fool 'bout freedom rave and rout,
Miss Liberty is grand nae doubt,
When well we use her,
But then, ye ken, the perverse nowt
Do aft abuse her!

A WORD TO THE CANADIAN WEEVIL.

Inscribed to R. McKenzie Esq., Sarnia, Ont.

YE graceless wheat-destroying weevil,
Rampageous as the very devil,
Can ony tongue be to you civil;
By day or night,
On waving crops ye feast and revel,
Afore our sight.

A' that we do, a' that we say—
Though sinners swear and christians pray,
Yet still ye dinna mind a strae,
Ye tak your meal;
Ye just gang pouncing on your prey,
And fill your creel.

Dame Nature is a jade most fickle,
When crops look as they'd take the sickle,
Ye hool the heart o' ilka pickle
Just in a night,
And leave the faners but a rickle—
O' chaff to dight.

Misquitos, and sic like sma' fry,
Their ways and haunts we can espy,
Mair mense than you, though unco sly,
We can them smash,
And soon make them at death's door lie
Wi' little fash.

But you, ye brutes! to wisest men
Ye are a thought beyond their ken,
Where ye come frae, the how and when
To fill your kites,
E'en Hind has failed a hand to len'
To set to rights.

Ane e'en would think that Dr. Gill,
Who tugs our hearts and reins wi' skill,
Would 'pound a posset or a pill,
To gar them scour,
Like Johnnie Cope frae Birslie hill,
Within the hour.

Stook upon stooks sent to the midden,
Full monie a heart wi' grief ye sadden,
Ye spoilt Peg Dale's concocted weddin'
Wi' Robbie Rue,
Wha hadna gear to buy providin',
And a' for you.

There's Tammie Turnip, autumn past,
A sheep's e'e at Meg Colwort cast,
But you, ye souls, cam' like a blast
Upon his grain:
He nailed an oath to the bed-post,
To sleep his lane.

A gown o' silk Kate Kailrunt wanted,
She thought how brawly she could flaunt it,
She asked her man if he wad grant it—
He gave a roar,
Then heels o'er head the poor man canted
And ne'er spak' more.

There's our auld neighbor Sandy Bran,
A better chield life ne'er began,
From empty barns headlang ran,
Plung'd through a swamp;
Next morn was found cauld, stiff and wan,
Strung on a stump.

A slee auld carl was Geordie Jack,
Ae e'en sax cradlers on did tak',
Next morn he wasna worth a plack;
Wi' down cast main
He made a bullet straight play whack,
Out through his brain!

When Tam, the tailor, 'gan to shear,
He keekit in to a wheat's ear,
He gaped! he stagger'd! then did steer
With reckless canter;
Some arsenic grains dashed in his beer,
Tam died instanter!

I had an honest, frugal aunty,
Wha wi' her man lived in a shanty;
Ae night she was fu' weel and canty:
Woe's me, alack!
Next morn her spirit took a jauntie,
And ne'er cam' back!

Such cases I might multiply,
All caused by that infernal fly,
How men, in scores, leap up sky high,
Wi' fear and fright,
And women groan, and faint, and cry
At dead o' night.

This business, sirs, must be corrected,
Losh me! the very nout's infected;
At stake and sta' they stand neglected,
    And hing their head,
E'en me, mysel', I'm sair dejected
    And near hand dead!

Ye men o' state! be up, be doin',
The cud o' strife no more be chewin',
No more intrig'in' plots be brewin';
    Wi' ae accord
Rise up! and save us a' from ruin,
    By fire or sword.

Ye cabinet men! lay heads thegether,
Bethink no more your nests to feather,
Stop for a space your dinsome blether,
    I speak ye civil,
Or if ye roar, roar a' thegether,
    And scare the weevil!

Let John McDonald seek them out,
Let Sandfield catch them by the cloot,
And a' the members roar and shout
    Wi' bellows lungs,
The very de'il himself you'd rout,
    To list your tongues.

I'll wager my auld bonnet blue,
A stot, a stirk, and forrow coo,
If ye just raise ae wild halloo
    'Mang the wheat crap,
The brutes will vanish like the dew,
    And ne'er come back!

The Cat Aneath the Chair.

AE night quo' Jock unto his wife, "atweel
I'll tak' a dander out ower to Mayshiel,
To speir if Will and a' the folk are weel."
Quo' Bess, "I wish ye'd stay wi' me to crack,
But if ye gang, I hope ye'll hurry back;
It's unco eerie when the stars appear,
To sit my lane and no ae neighbour near."
"For mercy's sake," quo' Jock, "the guid preserve us!
What's this o't now, losh! Bess, ha'e ye got nervous?
I'm e'en at my wit's end I maun to confess,
To find a cure to conquer your distress,
The buck-bean plant, the bark frae willow trees,
Might counteract and banish your disease;
The buck-beans, my auld grannie aft she blessed them,
They toned her nerves and strengthen'd up her system!
Sae if ye like, I'll rin wi' willing stride
And pu' that herbage frae the water side."
"Man, Jock," quo' Bess, "for guidsake stop your clavers,
It fairly scunners me to hear your havers!
Ye're growin' wise, losh, Jock! ye're byous clever
I sair misdoubt ye'll no be a lang liver."
At this Jock leugh, he ran to get his rung,
But was arrested by the guidwife's tongue;
Quo' she, "the like I ne'er saw a' my days!
Will ye gang that way? gang and change your claes,
Gae wash your face, and gi'e your hair a kame,
And e'en look purpose like when ye're frae hame,
See to your hair! I never saw the like,
Frae tap to tae ye're just a touzy tyke;
Man! if ye saw yersel' ye'd see a sight
Wad mak' ye swarf wi' downright fear and fright!

Look at your sleeve, your elbow through it keeks,
And guide us a', Oh! what a pair o' breeks!
As for your waist-coat and your very shirt,
I do declare they're just engrained wi' dirt!
Sax years by-gane ye was as clean's a preen,
A look o' you was pleasing to the een.
My certy! sic a change has now owerta'en ye
I think black burning shame to look upon ye!
I weel I wat whan ye to me cam' courtin',
Ye look'd a man wi' independent fortune;
Your hair lay sleek, your bannet stood a-jee,
Your ribbon-ends hung gracefu' 'bout your knee,
Ye were the wale—the pick o' a' the fallows,
Ye now look ripe and ready for the gallows!
A kind o' hang-dog look ye ha'e about ye,
That mak's my very soul at times mis-doubt ye;
Were ye dook'd in the burn, I ha'e my doubts
The water soon wad poison a' the trouts;
Get out my sight! redd up yersel', be quick,
Or thance I'll brain ye wi' the parritch stick!"
"Now Bess," quo' Jock, "when first I met wi' you,
Butter, I'm sure, wad no melt in your mou;
'Twas then I little dreamed that ye could flyte,
Yet still I trow your bark's worse than your bite."
With these remarks, forthwith a cannie tear
Did on the eyelash o' his wife appear,
Awhile it glisten'd, then sae mild and meek,
It fell and trickled o'er her rosy cheek;
Now Jock gaed up and clasped her to his bosom,
Then sair she rued that she did sae abuse him;
Now love and joy and pure domestic bliss,
Were centered a' in ae lang rousin' kiss.
And thus she spoke, "my words no tak' to heart,
Through fire and water, Jock, I'll tak' your part,
I wadna say an unkind word unto ye,
If wi' my heart and soul I didna lo'e ye."
Quo' Jock, "my dear, your council aye I prized."
Then aff he funked to do as was advised;

He soon gat ready—when the twasome parted,
They looked sae thowless and maist broken hearted!
But truth compels me here to write—maintain
That 'fore he left he kissed his wife again.
Jock's on the road; the reader now may learn
That Jock's guidwife is mother o' a bairn,
They trowed o' lasses fient a ane was wiser,
Guidfaith! the twa did fairly idolize her;
Wi' mickle care their wee bit pet they han'l'd—
She was their first, sae they were baith new fangl'd;
As sure's I breathe, it's near hand set me crazy
To list the uncos o' their wee bit Daisy!
Jock was a cannie, careless, drudging slunk,
But Bess was fou o' smeddum and o' spunk;
She'd wash and synd, and mak' and mend, and scour;
Perfection might ha'e dinner'd on her floor;
She had a job to tend and keep Jock right,
The loon somehow wad no stay in at night;
And aft she wished, like monie a girnin' dame,
He'd break his leg and then he'd stay at hame!
Then Mirth wad fill her heart up to the hilts,
When picturing Jock hung on a pair o' stilts;
Then Pity would arise as Grief drew near,
Then Hope would smile and wipe the pearly tear.
Now reader, if you please, we'll gang wi' Jock
And introduce ye to the Mayshiel folk.
"Whisht! bairns whisht, do stop that deavin' roar,
I hear a rap—there's some ane at the door,
As sure's I breathe, I'll gie my highest aith,
I canna hear a word aboon my breath,
Rin! Tammie, rin, and dinna snicker mair,
And pu' the bolt and see wha's standin' there.
Is that you Jock? guid save us, Jock, come in,
Guidwife, hang up John's bonnet on the pin;
How are ye man, and how is it a' wi' ye?
As sure as death I'm unco glad to see ye!
I haena seen your face for monie a day,
Man! ye're as welcome as the flow'rs o' May,

Come, draw your chair up to the ingle cheek;
Guidwife, just hang the kettle on the cleek:
Now bairns, awa to bed—ye noisy clips—
And if I hear ae word frae out your lips,
Ye'll get a something or I'm sair mista'en,
Will mak' your very banes roar out wi' pain!"
Wi' this the bairnies creepit ben the house;
Soon ower their glass baith Jock and Will sat crouse,
And Will's guidwife sat cosy by the ingle,
And at her stockin' she would crack and pingle,
Speir'd if Jock's wife had now gat weel again,
And if their Daisy yet could gang her lane?
Jock claw'd his head, awhile he humm'd and hackit,
Then said, "my wife's as weel's can be expeckit,
And our bit lass has now begun to toddle,
And o' her minnie just the very model;
She's unco sair been pester'd wi' her gums,
And a' the day bite biteing at her thum's,
She's tholed it weel, I'm glad to say that noo,
Twa teeth, like lances sharp, are keekin' through,
Hech me! I trowed that death awa wad ta'en her,
Whan the guidwife at first began to wean her,
She took the croup, and syne the scarlet fever,
The measles, faith! I thought they'd never leave her,
The measles! aft I've wished they were in Sodom,
They looked as if they wad ha'e dressed her drodum!
What next she'll tak' is mair than I can mention,
For that is something 'bune my comprehension!
Whate'er it is, we'll do our best to maister
Wi' drug and poultice, and wi' stickin' plaster."
"Aye, aye," quo' Will, "the ills o' life are monie,
We had an unco time wi' our wee Johnie,
He took a kind o' dwam and syne a quiver,
Guidfaith! we thought we'd loose him a' thegether!
We set to wark, we rubbed him wi' goose greese,
I do declare that soon did gie him ease;
And now-a-days the sumph believes our blethers,
And soon expects to raise a crap o' feathers!"

Wi' this Jock ga'e the table sic a bang,
He kicked, he roared and laughed baith loud and lang,
And Will's guidwife glower'd upward frae her stockin',
Then said, "guidman, I dinna like sic jokin',
Sic havers ! man, I'm sair inclined to doubt it,
That mickle guid ye winna see come out o't."
"Hoot toot," quo' Jock, "I'm unco sure, indeed,
He wadna wrang a hair on Johnie's head !
He's his ain flesh and blood in art and part,
I'm unco sure the bairn lies near his heart."
Wi' this the guidman handed Meg a glass,
And soon a smile cam' jinkin' on her face ;
The riseing laugh she did her best to burkit,
As round the corners o' her mouth it lurkit ;
Now as she listen'd to the men folks yaff,
She burstit out wi' ae lang glorious laugh !
She drap'd her wires and keek'd up in their faces,
And then she roared, "ye're just twa bletherin' asses !"
At times she held her sides, and 'tween her breath
She'd cry, "O ! stop, or else ye'll be my death !"
And then she'd rise and lean against the wa',
And beck and bow and vent the loud gaffaw.
At length she cried "guid guide us ! did ye ever !"
Then flung aside her stockin' a' thegether.
Care's lugs were cuffed, nae hole had he to hide in,
Sae aff he sulk'd, and Joy was left presidin'.
　　Now after sunshine storms will aft arise,
And lash the placid ocean to the skies,
And after mirth aft comes the bitter tear,
And after battles heroes quail wi' fear !
　　As Jock was sittin' nickerin' in his chair,
Terror and horror seized him by the hair !
His eyes rolled round, his nether lip did quiver,
His cheek grew wan, his very limbs did shiver.
At last he yelled, "Oh ! Will, the fiend infernal
Has somehow cruppin' in to my internal !
I ne'er took sic a turn in a' my life,
Guid save us, Will, Oh ! send for Bess, my wife."

Will roars, "Oh! Meg, rin, flee awa my bairn,
Ben to the fire and bring a red-het airn;
Oh! haste, be quick—I'll say the ten commands,
Oh! Jock, man, dinna dee amang our hands.
Where are ye now, man Jock, I at ye speer
Gif ye are gane, or gif ye yet are here,
Come! speak man, Jock, and tell us what's amiss?"
"I'm on the tap," quo' Jock, "o' great distress,
I feel as if ten cats were doon my thrapple,
I'm gaun quick, Nick has me in his grapple!
A finger post stands 'fore me like a wraith,
Which points into the very jaws o' death!"
Oh! Jock," roared Will, "Oh! dinna dee sae soon,
Here comes the airn, Meg! Meg! pull aff his shoon
And clap it to his feet, woes me, guidwife,
The airn het might bring him back to life."
Doon on the floor wi' speed the guidwife crap,
When fuff! a cat play'd wallop in her lap,
She gave a loup, then cried, "losh! I declare,
That cat, Oh! Jock, sprang out frae 'neath your chair;
Oh! tell us man if to the quick he's scratched ye,
Or if the deevlish brute's somehow's bewitched ye!"
"Deil tak' the wretch," roared Jock "I'd no be sweer
To open up his throat frae ear to ear!
The purrin' brute! may Nick do nought but singe him,
And pokers het in his vile carcass plunge them!
He's gi'en me sic a fright, I'm bound to say,
I'll ne'er get ower it to my deein' day!"
"Poor brute," quo' Will, "he was ane o' the party,
And did his best to croon and to divert ye."
"Divert me," quo' Jock,—Jock said what I'll no name,
He snatch'd his bannet, started for his hame;
And since that night, Jock never wander'd mair,
He ne'er forgot the cat aneath the chair!
And aye sin' syne when fools mis-uses life
And winna stay at hame aside their wife,
But spend the gear that should ha'e boilt the pat,
The wives will say, "I hope they'll hear the cat!"

TAM AND TIB; OR, CAUSE AND EFFECT.

Inscribed to James W. Weir Esq.

TAM and Tib sat by the fire,
And they began a crackin',
Quo' she, "guidman, I mind the day,
I could rin like a mawkin.'
But now I'm getting auld and stiff,
And unco sair forgesket,
I muckle doubt the hand o' death
Is fum'lin' 'bout my brisket!

"Last night I had a fearfu' dream,
My very blood seemed frozen,
I thought Auld Nick, on a black horse
Cam boundin' through the losin!
He had a night-cowl on his croon,
Through it twa horns ascended;
A cloak he had o' bumbazine,
Which to his hoofs descended.

"His tail was arched like the half moon,
And which stuck through his cloakin',
And Tam, as far's I could perceive,
'Twas langer than your stockin'.
His nose was flat, his chin was sma',
His lips stuck out between them,
Ye'd sworn his lugs were asses' lugs,
Guidman! if ye had seen them.

"His face was just as black's the crook,
    His een were halflins steekit,
And a' the hair aboot his beard
    Was scorched and brimstone smeekit.
His shoulder blades maist touched his jaws,
    His back was bent maist double,
He looked as if he had come through
    A whirlwind o' trouble.

"And sic a pair o' specks he wore,
    Wi' him ye wadna swapit,
Their wires were tied wi' woolen threads,
    And baith their een were crackit.
Tam, he seemed waff and broken doon,
    Condemned and disconcerted,
Yet still he tried his best to show
    He wasna broken hearted.

"I trowed his heart was worrit out
    Wi' planin' vile dissensions,
He yet seemed gash enough to coup
    Cart-loads o' guid intentions.
A glimmer o' a thought arose,
    Which through my harn-pan creepit,
That it was queer how a' our crimes
    Should on Nick's back be heapit.

"We dread I keekit in his face,
    Syne speared wha next he wanted?
He gae a spring frae aff his horse,
    Then heels-o'er-head he canted!
He bounced and bounded like a ba',
    Kists, chairs and stools he coupit,
He ga'e a roar, syne wi' a bang
    Right on my breast he loupit!

"'For mercy's sake,' I cried, 'get aff,'
    And syne I did implore him,
But ere I wist on my breast-bane,
    He danced up Tullochgorum!

His hoofs played clatter on my banes,
  His tail he lashed and flouted,
And in my lugs unearthly sounds
  And mockriff laughs he shouted.

"Man! how he reeled and how he flang
  Wi' perfect exhultation,
Till ilka pore was rinnin' out
  Wi' brimstone perspiration!
Out frae his mouth shot bolts o' fire,
  That gar'd me geck wi' wonder,
And when he shut his lantern jaws,
  They crackit like the thunder!

"At last he sprang upon his horse,
  Then cried, 'guidwife, instanter
Loup on a-hint, and you and I
  This night we'll ha'e a canter!'
Against my will he hauled me up,
  Tam! how my heart gaed thumpin'
When Auld Nick's horse began to snort,
  And syne began a-jumpin'.

"We flew o'er hill, we flew o'er dale;
  Auld Satan wasna idle,
He cracked his whip, he spured and spured,
  And ruggit at the bridle.
Then through amang the moons and stars
  We rode like desperation,
At last we nimbly lighted doon
  Upon a constellation!

"We stood upon a mighty cliff,
  Aside a raging river,
Then Satan roared and said, 'guidwife,
  Ye now are mine forever.'
I cried 'ye loon, stand back! stand back!
  I scunner at your caperin',
Losh guide us a', he made a grab
  And catched me by the apron.

"My blood boiled up, and when I yelled
Auld Nick was fair confounded;
I cam' a yerk upon his claws,
And frae his presence bounded!
I flew and flew, and better flew
Back to the earth did glide, man,
And when I woke, losh, guide us, Tam,
I e'en lay by your side, man!

"I'm unco sure that these are signs
That I maun leave ye soon, man,
Yet 'fore I'm earthed, I'd like to ken
Wha ye'll get in my shoon, man?"
Tam opened up his auld tin mull,
And he began a snuffin',
And then he said, "now, Tib, your lugs
Do weel deserve a cuffin'.

"We hae kent ane another lang,
We're unco weel acquainted;
And if ye dee, I'm bound to say
Mair wives will ne'er be wanted!
Yet still ye dinna look amiss,
Ye're fresh as ony daisy;
That unco dream I ha'e nae doubt
Has near-hand set ye crazy.

"Ne'er fash your thumb aboot Auld Nick;
Some say he's dead and chestit,
E'en Harry Beecher o' New York,
Contends he ne'er existit.
I ha'e a kind o' mither wit,
Though ne'er was a great scholar,
Yet I ha'e learned to prize twa laws—
The natural and the moral.

"Last night ye ken was hogmanay,
Ye loaded sair your crappin,
That was the cause, and the effect
Was unco sure to happin.

If folk wad lead a temp'rate life
In drinkin' and in eatin',
At night, wi' Satan and sic nowt,
They ne'er wad ca' a meetin'.

"And strive to learn that God is love—
Love and not dread our Maker,
And banish superstitions cant
'Bout hells black hallanshaker.
"Now guidwife gang and tak' a rest,
Lie cozie in your hammock,,
And learn a lesson frae last night,
Ne'er to o'erload your stomach."

Quo' Tib, "ye're good at an advice,
Your wisdom's deep's a well, man,
But Tam tak' tent, and e'en tak' hame
Your council to yersel', man."
Here Tammie ga'e a kind o' grunt,
And syne a wee he coax'd her;
It wasna lang e're she slept sound
And sweet aneath his oxter!

NAN O' LOCKERMACUS.

Inscribed to Graham Wilson, Esq., Bay City, Mich.

"Visions and magic spells can ye despise,
And laugh at witches, ghosts and prodigies."

In the long winter evenings, our ingle-side was often visited by an old shepherd, well known in the Lammermoors by the name of Auld Tam McCleish. Although verging, at that time, upon three score and ten, he was hale and hearty. He was a steadfast believer in the supernatural, and would unfold tales about bogles, ghosts, witches, warlocks, fairies, brownies, water-wraiths, kelpies and dead-raps that filled us with such fear and terror, that even while we listened, we were afraid to look over our shoulder, and some of us, rather than venture out in the darkness, would have preferred to be lashed within an inch of our lives Auld Tam always carried a long staff with an iron pike in the end of it, for the purpose of protecting himself from the attacks of the "Unco folk." He also carried in his pouch a kind of white snuff, which he called "witch powder," and if any of the cattle in the neighborhood got bewitched, he would blow, with a quill, some of the powder into their eyes, for the purpose of breaking the witch-spell. The powder he would also administer to human beings as occasion demanded. In the morning, if a hare happened to cross his path, he considered it unlucky, and would immediately return home and remain till the sun went down. He had a strong aversion to the pyet, *i. e.*, magpie; the following, regarding that bird, he was in the habit of repeating with awful solemnity:

"Ane's a waddin', twa's a birth,
Three's the dead-thraw, four is death."

There was an old woman in the village called "Witch Nan," for whom he also had a strong dislike. According to him, no one would dream a fearful dream or see a vision without Nan being, some way or another, at the bottom of it. If sickness came among the cattle, Tam was always ready, like a ministering angel, with his quill and powder; and if any of the cattle chanced to die, he would with frenzy exclaim, "May the deil row Nan in his blankit! She's beat me this time, but I hope I'll live lang enough to see day about wi' that lim' o' Satan." He seemed to consider that he held a commission to baulk Nan's evil machinations; in a word, to do his best to thwart her in her glamour-castings, spells and cantrips. After great persecution, Nan somewhat mysteriously left that part of the country, and Tam McCleish's occupation, like Othello's, was gone. He laid aside his staff, his quill and his witch powder, and drooped and died.

The following is an attempt to illustrate some of the notions that once prevailed regarding the "Unco folk."

LANGSYNE upon the Millwud brae,
A witch ance lived, as I've heard say,
A kind o' poor, decrepit crater,
The very picture o' ill-nater;
A' day at the fireside she'd cour,
A' night o'er hill and dale she'd scour,
And play sic cantrips far and near,
As filled baith auld and young wi' fear;
At night the bairns wad spring to bed,
And jerk the blankets o'er their head,
Syne trembling baith in lith and limb,
They'd pray, or croon their wee bit hymn;
Sair they wad strive to fa' asleep
Afore auld Nan would on them creep!

A couple liv'd south at Rawburn,
For snuff and tea sair they did girn;
Ae day their Bess was sent to Dunse,
To buy the tea and half an o'nce
O' snuff; whan she was coming back,
The shades o' night did her o'ertak',
She had win down the Henly-hill,
And safely gained and passed Blacksmill,
When wind began to blaw and rift,
And lightning flash across the lift;
The thunder bellowed o'er her head,
Bess tore alang wi' a' her speed;
Just as the storm began to lull,
A something ga'e her skirt a pull!
A something whispered in her ear,
That made her shake and quake wi' fear!
Syne like a dog around her reel'd,
And bark'd and whinged, and roared and squeel'd,
Amang her feet it ga'e a wallop,
Syne aff it scour'd wi' fearfu' gallop!
Poor Bessie roar'd, "Oh, guid keep me!"
Wi' dread she drop'd the snuff and tea;

Power fairly left her arm and hand,
And like a statue she did stand;
Then took leg bail wi' a' her might—
No earthly power could stop her flight!
As she gade springing o'er a mire,
There cam' a dazzling flash o' fire,
A something past her ga'e a rush,
Then dashed into a boortree bush!
Bess closed her e'en and lap the ditches,
To get scot free frae Nannie's clutches.

When she gat hame, I e'en may tell
How in her mother's arms she fell,
And swoon'd and fainted clean awa,
And when her lungs began to draw,
At intervals, she did relate
How Nan, the witch, had crossed her gait;
Her mother cried, "the deil tak' me,
Witch Nan has got my pickle tea!"
E'en Bessie's father took the huff,
His nose and mull were scant o' snuff;
I'm laith to say he swore an aith,
And thus he spak below his breath,
"I durstna fell Nan wi' this poker,
Yet still, I pray, the snuff will choke her.
There's nane in a' the rounds wad care,
Though she lay stiff for ever mair!"
Then they did brew for Bess some toddy,
To keep the spirit in her body.
For weeks poor Bess was pale and wan,
And a' the blame was laid on Nan.

Now Tam McCleish cam' round aboot,
He saw poor Bess as white's a cloot,
Wi' anxious care forthwith did try
To find out Bessie's malady!
He heard about her unco fright,
He said, "my dear, I'll set ye right,

I'll break Nan's spell, guidfaith ! my certy
I soon will mak' ye hale and hearty."
Now Tam did mix up a witch pouther,
Three times he flang some o'er her shouther,
Syne charged her weel whan night did fa',
To swallow down a grain or twa ;
But 'fore the spell wad fair be broken,
Two drachms she must tie in her stockin',
And after she had ta'en the dose—
To sup a hearty kit o' brose !
Afore he left, he charged them sair
To send him word how Bess did fare,
And if she wasna' gettin' better,
He'd tak' another guid look at her,
And, if he thought there was occasion,
He'd gi'e her mair examination !
Tam took his stick, bade them guid day,
And never stop'd for thanks or pay.

There was a man ca'd Andrew Luke,
Wha gaed to Dunse to hire a cook ;
Whan comin' hame ae Friday night,
Losh, me ! the twasome gat a fright !
The stars abune their heads were peepin'
As they alang the road were creepin' ;
(The cook was just a kind o' trollop,
They gade like twa snails at the gallop,
And Andrew didna' care a snap
To what extent she took her stap.)

He raised his voice, and thus did speak :
"My lass, whan hame, be sure to steek
And fasten weel your bedroom door,
Case Nan, the witch, should you devour."
Wi' this the cook did quick remark,
"That it was growing fearfu' dark."
"Ye're right," quo' he, "the deil be in it,
It's got pitch dark just in a minit."

Now down the hill runs a bit burn,
Just where the fit-road tak's a turn,
A gust o' wind wi' swirlin' speed
Did nearly knock them heels ower head!
Their very hearts lap to their mouth,
For, whan they ventured to gang south,
A brute just like a hoodie craw
Cam' swatt'ring in atween the twa!
It had a neb sax inches lang,
And frae its neb there shot a fang,
It had twa fiery wull-cat een,
It had twa legs baith lang and lean,
And aye it ga'e the ground a claw,
Then lap and danced around the twa,
And whiles it ga'e a curious craik,
That gar'd the cook and Andrew shake!
The cook sent forth an unco roar,
Then cried, "Oh! shut my bed-room door."
She gave a spring, then aff did birr,
While Andrew no ae fit could stir.

It just was striking twa o'clock,
Whan Andrew at his door did knock,
"Wha's at the door?" his wife did cry;
"I think it's me," was his reply.
Then up she rose to let him in,
He, like a ghost, did past her spin,
In hole and corner he did look,
At length he cried, "where is the cook,
The diel a bit o' me can see her,
Oh! what on earth ha'e ye done wi' her?"
Quo' she, "Guidman, ye're clean gane daft,
The fient a cook cam' ower the craft."
He lifted up his hands on high
"May heaven protect us!" he did cry,
"As sure as death, we may depend,
This warld is coming to an end,
It winna do just now to swear,
For losh! our ends are drawing near!"

Next morn, like fire, the story ran,
How that infernal witch, ca'd Nan,
Had turned hersel' into a craw,
And Andrew's cook had witch'd awa !
Folk sought the lass, but fient a hair
O' her on earth was e'er seen mair.
Andrew ae night keek'd through Nan's losin,
At the fireside he saw her dosein',
A cat was sitting on her back,
It purred but no a word Nan spak.
He tald the folk what there he saw,
And then he fainted clean awa,
But time has left no trace or track
To tell if Andrew's wind cam' back !

There lived out ower upon the common,
A kind of antiquated woman ;
Whan she was young, she had got married,
But death her guidman aff had carried ;
And now she kept a coo or twa
An' sold the milk in Randyraw,
Now, this guidwifie's nomenclater,
I e'en may tell—was Peggy Frater,
She sang a' day like a canary,
And trig and clean she kept her dairy,
She hadna' muckle warld's wealth,
But she was strong, and had her health.

Ae day the bairnies in the Raw,
Did on their parritch fuff and blaw,
And some o' them did glunch and pout,
As Peggie's milk that morn ran out.
Next morn she cam' wi' pitious wail,
And tald an unco waesome tale :
" How her best coo had turned ill,
And wadna gi'e o' milk, a gill."
Quo' she, " I'm unco wae to think
That she now lies upon death's brink,

8

Though I did gi'e her fellin' grass
To help her through wi' her distress;
It fills my heart to hear her groan,
She's lying now down in the loan,
Her hours a very child might number,
She'll soon fa' into her last slumber;
I'm seeking now for Robie Baumer,
To fell her wi' his muckle hammer;
It's best to put her out o' pain,
For she'll ne'er be a coo again."
Wi' grief poor Peg began a-slotterin',
And aff for Robie she gade hotterin';
As she alang the doors did bellow,
Loud Tam McCleish did to her hallow;
He kindly speer'd at Mrs. Frater,
What gard her tears run down like water?
Then she did tell him wi' a hurry,
The cause o' a' her grief and flurry;
It didna tak' a lang oration
To let Tam ken her hale vexation.
Quo' Tam, "it will be a bad job,
If death frae you that coo should rob,
She has a bonnie head o' horns,
Their ends are just as sharp as thorns;
I wat, she is a beast well made,
Her legs are sma', her brisket's brade,
Her hide is just as saft as silk,
And what a jaw she gi'es o' milk,
Her skim milk's grand, I do declare it,
The mair I'd drink, I'd drink the mair o't!
And than the cream, I do believe it,
Is just the thickness o' a diviot,
Her butter, aye, guidfaith, indeed,
Its marrow ne'er was spread on breed!"
Tam thought awhile and then did say,
"We e'en will dander up the brae,
I'll tak' a look at her, ma fegs,
And try to set her on her legs,

Another tear now dinna drop,
Guidwife! as lang's there's life, there's hope!"
"Weel," quo' the wife, "yet I'll maintain,
That a' our efforts will be vain,
Man! Tam, if ye but heard her blaw
Ye'd trow she was in the dead-thraw."
Tam drew his hand frae out his pocket,
His bonnet on his head he knockit,
Then up the brae did meditate,
Till they gat through the plantin' gate;
Syne aff they waded through the clover,
Fu' kind and couthie wi' ilk other;
The winds were blawing saft and sweet,
The flowers were blooming 'mang their feet,
Up in the air the larks were springing,
The birdies on ilk tree were singing,
The lambs upon the knowes were dancing,
Down on the burn the sun was glancing;
As Tam did look at Mrs. Frater,
He said, "how grand's the works o' nater."
"Aye, aye," quo she, "I'm sure I'd feel
Contented if ma coo was weal,
O' care and grief we'll ha'e our load,
Sae lang as we're abune the sod,
And though my coo do run her race,
I'll get another in her place;
I'd ance a hantle mair to mourn,
Whan my guidman was frae me torn,
For, whan his spirit gaed aboon,
Nae ane on earth could fill his shoon."
Fu' cosh they crack'd for half a mile,
Until they reached the auld dyke stile;
As o'er the steps they singly creepit,
And on the other side they drepit,
They saw the coo lie in the loanin',
And loud and lang the beast was groanin';
Then Tam gade round and round about her,
Quo' he, "I unco sair misdoubt her,

I maistly think 'twill be in vain
To raise her on her legs again."
And then he cockit up his eye,
And said, "we might do worse than try."
Down in the ground his stick he stapit,
He placed his bannet on the tap o't,
As fou as it would hold, the quill
Wi' pouther he did deftly fill;
To the guidwife he said at length,
"Just grip her tail wi' a' your strength,
And in a minit I will tell,
If I ha'e broken Nannie's spell."
Peg held the tail—at the cow's head
Tam louted down wi' spraicklin' speed,
Whiff in her e'en the pouther blew,
She roared, then to her feet she flew,
And o'er Tam's body ga'e a spring,
While to the tail the wife did hing.
Tam yelled, "the deil's got in the coo!
Hech me! I'm fairly done for noo!"
He thought the beast wad fair devour him,
As the auld wife played yerk out ower him.
At length Tam to his feet did whip,
And on the knowe he ga'e a skip,
"That coo," quo he, "will soon be well,
Losh, me! I've broken Nannie's spell."
Now, Mrs. Frater cried, "alack!
Ye've broke the spell an' broke my back!"
But Tam ne'er cared a word she said,
He took his stick and aff he gade;
The guidwife rose, she heaved a sigh,
She saw her coo wi' tail on high,
Thundering alang wi' break-neck speed,
Tossing and shaking horn and head!
She thought, as it o'er dykes did bleeze—
The cure was worse than the disease!

There was a lad ca'd Jemmy Deans,
A lad possessed o' mense and means;
A horse unto a cart he yokit,
Then placed ten shillings in his pocket,
And aff he rode at mornin's sun,
To buy some coals—say half a ton.
While comin' hame on the auld track,
James Deans ahint the cart did walk;
The day was edging down to night,
The sun had gane clean out o' sight,
And darkness cam' sedate and still
And settled upon Harden's-hill.
When comin' past the Snuffy-holes,
James sprang upon the cart o' coals,
Put forth his hand the reins to catch,
But fient a rein was there to snatch;
He jumpit down and aff did stridle,
And caught the horse fast by the bridle,
To stop the beast he roar'd, "woa, woa!"
Yet still the horse wad onward go!
He looked a-head, what he saw there
Did mak' him gaze wi' idiot stare!
He saw a curious looking crater,
Just like a goat in shape and stature;
Twa horns frae out its skull ascended,
A beard far past its knees descended.
James Deans then swarfed wi' fear and fright,
On ilka horn he saw a light
That bleezed and burned bright and clear,
And sent a glimmer far and near!
At ilka step the brute wad take,
Its shaggy tail did toss and shake,
It held the reins fast wi' its teeth,
And pulled as if 'tween life and death.
Now Jemmy steevely held his whip,
He sprang and ga'e it sic a clip,
It drop'd the reins and up did spurt,
Backward it bleezed o'er horse and cart,

It bounded twenty feet or mair,
It turned and tumbled in the air,
From mouth and nostril forth there came
A red sulphurious blast of flame!
James stood and gazed with wild surprise,
Till fear shut up and sealed his eyes,
And when he opened them once more
He gave a wild unearthly roar—
He saw the brute plunge in the mire,
And vanish in a flash o' fire!
When James gat home he did report
How he made Satan loup and snort,
But folk about the Randy-raw
Did better ken what Jimmy saw;
They shook their heads with sore affliction,
Their thumbs did point in Nan's direction!

Ae night McCleish sat by the fire
Weavin' the thread around the wire;
A pair o' brogues lay 'neath his seat;
His slipshod bauchels graith'd his feet,
His bannet blue hung on a pin,
His cowl was strapped aneath his chin;
On his chair-back a plaid was hingin',
Out ower his head twa hams were swingin',
His staff lay on the dresser head,
Aside a trencher fou o' bread;
A cat lay beekin' in the nook,
The kettle sang upon the crook,
Upon the fire the peats were heapit,
Clean as a preen the hearth was sweepit,
His bellowses had blawn a gale—
They now hung breathless on a nail;
An ulzie lamp stood on the brace,
Wha's light shone shimmerin' on his face;
Tam at his stockin' sat and ply'd,
At times the canty fire he eyed,

And whiles he'd glow'r aboot asklent—
The very picture o' content.
Upon a shelf a mouse crap out,
It nibbled at auld Tam's dish-cloot:
The cat ne'er fashed to turn her e'e,
But looked as mim as mim could be;
McCleish now laid aside his stockin',
He raxed his pipe—began a smokin',
And like the bonnie female gender,
He placed his cloots upon the fender.
Then, like his drowsy cat, sat blinkin',
Till sleep upon his eyes cam' jinkin'.
    Now at this hour a graceless laddie
Wha was neglected by his daddie,
Straevaget round aboot that night
And in Tam's window saw a light;
He sleely mounted the door-stane,
And keekit through the window-pane;
And as he listen'd at the losin,
He heard that Tam was soundly dozein';
As Tam ga'e ae confounded snore,
The callant sleely op'd the door;
On tip-toe ben the house he slunk,
His een glanced on a brimstone spunk,
Its end he lit, then canny goes
And hauds it under Tammie's nose,
Then out the door awa gaed bleezin',
Afore McCleish began the sneezin';
Tam had some bristles in his beek,
And when the hair began to reek
He ga'e ae bound up in the air,
He yelled and raved wi' black despair,
He reeled and chok'd, he swore and swat,
He fuffed and paw'd just like a cat,
And when he drew a canny breath,
In vengeance wild he swore an aith—
He swore by moon and stars sae bright,
He'd murder Nan that very night!

Yes! 'fore the night wad steal awa',
He'd hew her up in pieces sma',
And throw her banes ahint the dyke,
For dogs and corbie-craws to pyke,
And ere he took a second thought,
A sword frae 'hint the bed he brought,
His ulzie lamp he quick blew out,
Syne to the passage aff he put;
But mischief's horn that night was fou,
For in the entry lay a soo;
Out ower its body auld Tam bounded,
Tam and the brute were fair confounded,
It ga'e a bloody, murdering roar,
Syne plunged out ower him to the door!
Tam turned as stiff and cauld as lead,
Then swarf'd away wi' perfect dread;
And when he rose he stood aghast,
He thought ilk breath wad be his last,
His bosom heaved with pangs o' grief,
He trembled like an aspen leaf,
Though hope revived he said, "dod blast it,
My days are gane, my life's exhausted,
My kane is paid—I'm here nae langer,
Yet still I'm like to burst wi' anger;
A bat or moudiwart might see
Nan soon will be the death o' me!"
That night Tam didna venture out,
He rowed his nose up in a cloot,
And 'mang his blankets shook wi' fear,
In case Witch Nan would re-appear.
While horror at his heart was snappin',
Despair was worrying at his crappen.
At length the mists o' morn departed,
And Tam arose sair disconcerted;
Though unco waff-like and forlorn,
He busket up at screigh o' morn,
Put on his shoon and eke his claes,
Syne doon the road he took his ways;

At ilka step his wrath increased—
It burned and simmer'd in his briest;
O'er dyke he glow'r'd, then roared "dod-rat-us,
There's the auld Endor howkin' 'taties!"
And as he thus a blink did hover,
His wrath was fairly boiling over;
He raised his voice and cried, "ye limmer,
Ye ne'er will see the flowers o' simmer;
Ye're on the verge o' the next warl',
Your banes I'll burn up in a barrel,
Langsyne by rights, ye scorpian woman,
'Mang seas o' fire ye should be soomin',
But faith this morn ye'll get your sneesh,
Or than my name's no Tam McCleish,
Your end is near, wi' Nick no doot
Ye'll soon be suppin' soup aboot!"
Nan roared, "gang hame, ye hoary ass,
Gang hame, and hide your ill-faur'd face,
Gang hame, ye wuzzent, slinkin' brock,
And tie your head up in a pock,
Ye menseless, mis-begotten tyke,
How dare ye venture ower my dyke,
And set your fit on my kail yard—
Ye gruesome tanker backit caird?
Gif ye a herrin's length come near me,
Just like a salmon trout I'll spear ye!"
Nan shook the grape, then cried, "ye nowt
Come on and get your harns dug out."
Tam cried, "ye brimstone hag o' Sodom,
Last night ye nearly dressed my drodum,
Ye witch notorious! dinna stare
As if ye didna ken or care,
Ye needna growl and girn wi' rage—
Ye've now attained a ripe auld age,
Steek baith your een, and haud your breath,
And be prepared for instant death!"
Nan stood erect, her foe she eyed,
With burning rage she thus replied—

"Big bolts of fire descend and cleave him!
Open ye earthquakes to receive him,
Engulph him in your dark abodes,
'Mang lizards, spiders, wasps and toads;
May vipers twist and coil around him,
May waters rush and fires confound him,
May noises ring and clash and clatter,
May terror turn his blood to water,
While monsters lash him to and fro
May pity never hear his woe!"
Tam stood stock still, for he did spy
Ten thousand furies in her eye.
He hung his head like a blate wooer,
Or rather like an evil doer;
Her words, a metaphor to borrow,
Did prick him to the very marrow;
Although his knees did shake and tremble,
His fears he tried hard to disemble;
And thus he spoke: "Nan, say nae mair,
Else frae the roots I'll rive your hair;
Woman, I'll gi'e ye sic a mell,
Will crack your skull like an egg shell,
And ere your lugs are done wi' ringin',
I'll peel your hide aff like an ingan;
Last night ye filled me fou o' pain,
But now your day o' grace is gane,
Ye needna stand and shake and shiver,
Ye can't expect to live forever!"
Tam ga'e a glower and syne a gape,
Then cried, "ye randy, drap that grape;
Losh bliss my soul, that's byous queer,
I've e'en forgot baith sword and spear!"
Then Nannie cried, "Tam, come your ways,
And get the length o' the grape taes;
Will ye no come? by a' that's true
I soon will be the death o' you!"
She gave a spring, Tam turned his heel,
While Nannie after him did squeel,

He bicker'd like the very wind,
And left poor Nannie far behind.
He keekit round, then cried, " ye witch ye,
I'd think black burning shame to touch ye."
Nannie stood snirtin' in her sleeve,
And unto proud o' her reprieve.
Now Tam McCleish did hameward snool,
As dowf and docile as a mule,
Which tells the aft repeated tale,
That nought 'gainst woman can prevail;
By hook or crook on a' occasions,
She's master o' the situations.
Twa weeks gade by wi' cannie speed,
Nae reek cam' out Nan's chimbly head,
By day or night the ne'er a ane
Had seen or heard her mak' a din.
At last they ventured to her biggin',
They dug a hole clean through the riggin',
Back to the earth they lap wi' fright,
For, Oh! they saw an unco sight!
They saw Nan drawn np twa fauld,
And lying dead, and stiff and cauld.
Next day they bursted in her door,
They stared and still they wondered more,
Nan's cat stood there wi' glowerin' een,
But ne'er a shred o' Nan was seen!
Then up stood ancient Tam McCleish,
And after he had ta'en a sneesh,
He said, "last night when down the haugh,
O'er head I heard an eldrich laugh,
I gazed right up and there I saw
Twa witches airtin' for Dunse law!
The tane had on a blood red mantle,
Wi' flannel toy tied on her cantle;
The other's face was sour and crabbit,
And she had on a ridin' habit;
I'm unco sure this ane was Nannie—
She looked sae wud and sae uncanny.

I stood, I gazed wi' abject wonder
To see them cleave the cluds asunder,
They joukit here, and whirl'd there,
They tossed and tumbled in the air;
At times they high o'er head gaed springin',
Syne round the circle they gaed swingin';
Auld Nan, the base black hearted jade,
Seemed dext'rious at the fleeing trade,
The hag, the bleezing Satan's limb,
Appeared to be in glor'ous trim;
They baith were in the highest feather,
They played and friskit wi' ilk other;
'Twad gien a very saint the frantics
To ha'e observed their deevilish antics;
Ance they drew near, and by my faith
I thought fu' sure I'd be their death!
My gun wi' muckle speed I cockit,
The stock I to my shoulder lockit,
I took an aim, and I'll be bound
The twa wad soon ha'e kissed the ground,
I'm unco sure they'd got their clink,
If they had hover'd just a blink,
If they had tarried for the shot
I'm sure I'd blawn baith to pot!
But guide us a'! there's monie a slip
Tak's place between the cup and lip;
The gun struck back wi' sic a jar
Which knock'd me endways 'mang the glaur;
And as I groaned wi' bitter spite,
The twasome flaffered out o' sight!"
Then a' the folk cried, "guid forsake us,
Nan's weel awa frae Lockermacus!"
Witch Nan is gane! the dominie chuckle
He's yerkit superstitions knuckles,
He, with the aid o' press and pu'pit,
Has Witch and Warlock fairly routit!
And wisdom cries, "their loss is gain,"
To which the Bard writes down—Amen.

THE POOR O' THE PARISH.

Inscribed to W. Brack, Esq., Duntroon, Ont.

THE Poor o' the Parish are mickle to main,
In a *but* or a *ben* they dwall by their lane;
Their friends are but few, and but little they care
How the auld bodies fend or the auld bodies fare.
The back-end o' life e'en has mickle to dree;
The youthfu' ne'er dream what auld age has to see,
The warld's vain hopes in their bosoms they cherish,
They ne'er ha'e a thought being Poor o' the Parish.

The Poor o' the Parish are laden wi' care,
Their eldin's but scant and their cleedin's but bare;
Yet they grudge nae the rich wha in luxury shine,
But blest wi' contentment they never repine.
There's auld Eppie, poor body, she works at her stockin',
On the gate o' the grave, wi' eild she is rockin',
In her Bible she reads—it's a' that can nourish
The hearts o' the weary, the Poor o' the Parish.

She gangs to the kirk cleedit barely eneugh,
But her heart is weel clad wi' the robes o' the truth,
Aft doon her wan cheek the silent tears fa',
As she hearkins o' Him wha died for us a'.
Her bairnies that's livin' are awa like the frem'd,
The guidman o' her bosom death langsyne has claim'd,
But there's *ane* ever near—never backward to cherish
And comfort the weary—the Poor o' the Parish.

9

She hopes soon to dwall in the mansions above,
Where the poor are made rich through a Saviour's love,
Where nae sorrow can enter, nae grief can oppress,
Where a' is ae day o' unchangeable bliss.
Aye, there's *ane* high aboon wha kens a' our ken,
What we gi'e wi' our heart it's to *Him* that we len',
Folk, dinna be scrimp, 'twill gi'e life a relish,
To be couthie and kind to the Poor o' the Parish.

To James Walker, Esq., Detroit.

Sir :—

LAST night I took an unco turn,
Death nearly caught me in his girn,
Man ! I did think my earthly pirn
Had run its course ;
At length I'm round this morning stirrin',
No muckle worse !

By spells I thought it was the ague,
By jerks I thought it the lumbago,
"Het saut," I cried, "frae Onondaga,
Rub on! rub on !
Jee ! fly for doctors on a nagie
Afore I'm gone !"

Sae soon as I wi' speech was dune,
A whirling I took in my croon ;
I trow'd my breeks and my auld shoon
Nae mair I'd fill,
I bade farewell to knife and spoon
And sneeshin' mill.

My pores at length began a rinnin'
On bowster, blanket, cod and linen,
And 'fore the doctors a' cam' spinnin'
        My een to close,
I gather'd strength to put a spoon in
        And sup some brose.

And then to a' I did rehearse—
Sometimes in prose, sometimes in verse—
How folk that's born about the Merse
        Are strong and hardy;
So friends ye needna yoke the hearse
        Yet, for the Bardie!

With this they a' with laughter fought;
The guidwife cried, "losh, I forgot
To tie my stocking round your throat—
        There! dearest rest."
Her thankful tears fell burning hot
        Upon my breast.

Then Hope did bark and worry fear,
Then gentle sleep came cantering near,
And when the morning sun shone clear
        I ope'd my eyes,
And found, that I, your friend, was here
        Below the skies!

Now, Walker, if the day keep fine,
And if the sun no cease to shine,
Expect me at your house to dine,
        'Tween sax and seven;
Meanwhile, I am, in friendship—thine
        Sae lang's I'm livin'.

To Dad Brichan, Esq.

Wha cam' to Detroit, and wha left in a hurly burly; and wha gat his fiddle broken, and then to mak' amends began to sing; and wha scoured the conntry far an' near to get the sang beginning wi' the words—

"My name is Bauldy Fraser, man,
I'm puir, an' auld, an' pale, an' wan,
I brak my shin, an' tint a han'
Upon Culloden lea, man!"

He gat the sang, and if his wind-pipe no get crackit like his fiddle, he will sing it in grand style to his many friends and admirers at Petrolia, Ontario, on St. Andrew's day.

MY honest, bletherin', canty Dad,
Gosh, whan ye cam', man, I was glad,
But, like a March hare I was mad
Whan I did hear
That ye had row'd about your plaid,
And aff did steer.

Did police loons threat to arrest ye,
Did petticoated jades molest ye,
Or what in a' the earth possessed ye
To tak' leg bail
And rin as if Auld Satan chased ye
Doon to the rail?

Though I consider ye did wrang,
Yet still I send ye up the sang,
And hope ye will be in the fang
To scraugh away,
And sing it weel your friends amang,
On Andrew's day.

Now, Dad, I'm unco laith to say,
Wi' you I canna meet that day,
To hear ye sing, and screed and pray,
An' laugh and joke,
As I maun stap to ha'e my say,
Wi' our ain folk.

But whan the snaw is aff the grund,
And whan the spring blaws out her wind
I'll wager you ae sterling pund
I'll no be slack
To tak' a cannie dander round
Wi' you to crack.

I hope and pray that ye'll attend it,
And get your guid auld fiddle mendit,
And no again awa to lend it
To some fule bairn,
And get it ance mair rack'd and rendit,
Frae stem to stern.

And whan I come, ye'll yerk the strings,
Sae grand ye'll play the Highland springs,
Wi' glee we'll mak' the very tings
Get up and scour,
And jump and flee as if they'd wings,
About the floor!

As sure's I breath, I here declare,
Whan ye play up a Scottish air,
The first note cracks the croon o' care,
The second line
Just mak's ma twa een glint an' glare
Wi' joy divine!

I've seen whan I was fairly blockit,
And no ae penny in my pocket,
To buy my breakfast or my nocket,
And friends were scanty,
My harp! losh, man, I up wad tak' it,
And soon got vauntie!

I didna grumble, girn and clatter,
And hing my lugs about the matter,
But wi' the Muses aff I'd blatter,
An' loup care's hurdles !
And left the jade ahint, dod rat her,
Wi' other mortals.

Now fare ye weel, my fiddlin' daddie,
Gi'e my respects to your fair lady,
I hope ye row her in your plaidie
In this cauld weather,
An' at the fireside brew the toddy,
Fu' crouse thegether.

I hope that Buckham's skill and washes
Ha'e gard ye smash your goggle glasses,
And that nae mair ye'll tak' out passes
And ride to Flint,
And get your een row'd up wi' messes
O' lard and lint.

I hope ye'll lang enjoy your smoke,
And in your chair fu' cheerie rock,
And sing a sang, and crack a joke—
My Niff-naff carle,
And pu' your fiddle out the pock
And gar her skirl.

This warld is whiles a perfect staw,
Care comes wi' ilka breath we draw,
If 'twere na for a friend or twa—
You're ane believe it,—
I wadna care a single straw
How soon I'd leave it.

Now, Dad, I trust that whan we die,
We'll ha'e nae trouble in the sky,
But on the wings o' glory fly,
Wi' a' our might,
Where we will neither grieve nor sigh
'Mang realms o' light !

The Second Sight.

Inscribed to H. Moffat, Esq. "A man o' the Merse."

Though the fairies and bogles have vanished, yet there remain believers in what is termed in Scotland the "second sight." Those who possess this gift, as far as I can understand, somewhat resemble the "Medium" of the Spiritualists. Though the author is no believer in the supernatural, yet candor compels him to state that the main incidents in the tale, as told by "Uncle John," are truthfully related. I may also remark that the spot where the ghost of the gifted student appeared, has been often pointed out to the writer of these lines.

THE wintry winds were blawing unco sair,
The trees stood shivering wi' their branches bare,
A goustie night set in—the angry blast
Was howling fiercely frae the east to wast.
Auld Uncle John was sitting on the bunk,
Lunting his cutty wi' a brimstone spunk;
The fire upon the hearth was bleezing bright—
A couthie comfort in a cauldriff night,
A stack o' peats stood up ahint the byre,
We didna fail to kittle up the fire;
Now my auld grannie round the house was splutterin',
And to hersel some unkent words was mutterin',
And as the blast wi' vengeance sair was leatherin',
She e'en sat down and thus began a bletherin':—
"'Twas just a night like this, whan in my youth,
I then was living wast at Horseupcleugh,
The snaw, knee deep, baith hill and dale did cover,
The mountains seemed to groan to ane another,

The ice had spang'd and frozen pool and burn,
And a' the yird was just as hard as airn,
The icicles in ranks, in fronts and rears,
Hung down like daggers, swords, and pointed spears,
The wind in blasts gade whistling through the lane,
The hailstanes clatter'd 'gainst the window pane,
As sure as death at times we swarf'd wi' fright
I weel I wat, it was a judgment night!

"My neighbor lass was bonny Betty Broon,
As nice a lass as ever step'd in shoon!
Her een were just a shade 'tween black and blue,
Red were her cheeks, like cherries was her mou';
I eke may say, at mornin' or at e'en,
Out doors or in, she aye look'd trig and clean;
She sang sae sweet, she aye was blyth and gash,
Sae gallant gade, an' stood as streight's a rash!
And a' the lads, baith far and near, allow'd
That Betty's hair was like the links o' gowd!

"She had a lad that liv'd at Cranshaw toon,
Wha thought the warld o' his ain Betty Broon,
A gentle lad, he neither drank nor smokit,
And Bet and he wi' fond endearments trockit;
They had agreed to marry 'bout the Lammas,
An' tak' up house somewhere aboot Auld Cammas,"
To be particular (Grannie then did say),
That Betty's sweetheart was ca'd Sandy Hay.

"Twa men folk we had likewise in the ha',
Ane ca'd Tam Dodds—the other Jamie Shaw,
Out bye the wark was ower aboot the toon,
Horses were supper'd an' were bedded doon,
The kye had a' been look'd to in the byre,
And we sat crackin' round the kitchen fire.
Tam Dodd was weak in head but strong in lung,
He never kent the way to hold his tongue,
I've threaten'd aft to tear it frae the root,
I'm unco sure, in twa, 'twad clip'd a cloot,

There's nought on earth wad stop his dinsome blether,
Out o' a hair the ass wad mak a teather!
He'd jeer and jaw and say sic silly things,
I e'en ha'e sworn to fell him wi' the tings!
But, as I said afore, we a' sat crackin',
Out bye the storm did no appear to slackin'.
Tam Dodds gade out, but soon cam clotterin' back,
He shook wi' cauld and in the nook he crap,
'Hech me,' quo he, 'the storm does roar and rift,
Ye canna see a styme for sleet and drift,
The night is dungeon dark, hech! how it blows,
I couldna see an inch afore my nose!'
"And then he said to Betty, 'noo, ma woman,
I trow this night your jo' will no be comin',
If he should venture out frae Cranshaw toon,
He ne'er again will see his Betty Broon!
He'll founder 'mang the haggs, or else, ma feigs,
He'll break his neck out ower the Raven-craigs!'
'Tam Dodds,' quoth I, 'lock up your tinkler jaw,
Or else I'll drive your head against the wa'.'
At this the blockhead chuckled in his glee,
'Wha kens,' he cried, 'but Betty wad tak' me.'
Now Betty turned as mad—her een did flare,
Quo' she, 'now, Tam, for guidsake sae nae mair,
I wadna ha'e (her face gat red wi' anger)
E'en your hale bouk for my jo's little finger!'
Now Betty rose an' e'en gade ben the ha',
I heard a scream, and then I heard a fa',
I hurried ben, and there poor Betty lay,
Pale as a ghost an' a' her breath away!
I ran for water wi' a pell-mell race,
And deftly dash'd it on her brow and face.
Right glad was I, and thankfu' too, I ween,
Whan light began to glimmer in her een;
I raised her up and set her on a chair,
And O! how drench'd was a' her gowden hair,
The whiteness o' the lily left her face,
The blushing rose took up the lily's place,

And then she spoke, and oh! she spak sae wae,
I'll mind her words unto my dying day.
She said, as she gade up to her bit kist,
Afore her een there cam' a hazzie mist,
She saw her Sandy on the Felcleugh-law,
Wand'ring sae weary 'mang the trackless snaw,
She saw him stand, wi' looks o' wild despair,
He fell, she thought, to rise for never mair!
"What stuff," said I, "come now, gang to your bed,
That gouk, Tam Dodds, your fancy has misled."
But oh! waes me! unto the ha' next day
There cam' a man to seek for Sandy Hay,
His track was found—there on the Felcleugh-law
They found the poor lad perished 'mang the snaw,
Just at the spot where Betty saw him fa'!"

Then uncle John laid canny doon his pipe,
And wi' his sleeve a tear away did wipe,
And then he scratch'd an' scarted at his croon,
Then said to Grannie, "how cam' on Bet Broon?"
Then Grannie said, "for monie a day an' year,
She grat and mourned for him she held sae dear;
In life they loved, in death the twa were pair'd—
They sleep together in the auld kirk yard!"

My Uncle John then said "'twas strange and queer
How Sandy's ghost should to Bet Broon appear,
Your story, Grannie, ca's up to my mind
A circumstance o' the same kith and kind:
I mind fu' weel—'twas in the thirty-twa,
I then was living up at East Scarlaw,
My neighbor herd, I wat, was Andrew Reid,
As guid a man as e'er possessed a head,
As guid a herd as ever lampt the heather,
And he and I were unco grit thegether.
Now Andrew had a wife, her name was Tibby,
An honest, decent, weel respected body,
They had ae son, a weel far'd thrivin' bairn,
He was a genius—how the lad wad learn;

E'en at the table, when he supped his brose,
'Tween ilka sup the book was at his nose.
He gade to schule—his parents fondly hopit
They'd live to see his head wag in a pu'pit,
And when the dominie crammed him fu' o' knowledge,
They sent him aff to Edinboro' college.
And aft we heard that John was never beaten,
When he stood up to blether Greek and Latin,
Now ae professor tried John sair to tickle,
And put to him some questions hard and kittle;
John had him there! for just as quick as thought
The ready answer back to him he shot!
The great professor ga'e an unco stare,
Then speered at him where he had got his lair?
Then John stood up, and answered him fu' cool,
That he'd been taught at Lockermacus school;
The learned man ne'er tried again to puzzle him,
He soon found out that John could fairly muzzle him!
"Atween the sessions, John wad aye come hame,
To read and write, and rant and rave, and raim;
He'd rise and preach till he was like to choke,
He'd stand and pray unto his mother's clock!
Speak 'bout coal measures, quartz and chucky-stanes,
'Bout fossil plants, fish fins and herrin' banes,
And strive to show, by inferance and conjecture,
That Adam was of recent manufacture,
Else his remains, upon investigation,
Would have been found in some far back formation.
And that of Eve, our poor deluded mother,
The ne'er a hair o' her can man discover.
Now monie a time I thought his clash and clavers
Were just a pack o' senseless silly havers—
Bothering his brains about the warld's formation,
Instead of thinking 'bout his soul's salvation;
'Twould be far better if such men would try
To teach mankind to live, and how to die—
Point to the future—do their best to find
Some plan or project to improve mankind.

John wander'd 'mang the hills to rax his legs,
And gather'd weeds, stanes, beetles, fleas and clegs;
He piled the stanes in cairns in the garret,
He'd tell ye a' their names just like a parrot.
His father sometimes laughed fu' lang and crouse,
And say, 'John's rocks wad yet bring down the house.'
Although he had some crotchets in his head,
He was as kind a lad as e'er brak bread;
The minister e'en said, wi' muckle pride,
'John was a credit to the country side!'
And e'en the Laird's weel tocher'd daughter Nancy,
Confessed that John had fairly won her fancy,
At the kirk-door, or where she had a chance,
She'd nod her head, and kindly to him glance,
E'en at the prayers she wad stand wi' grace,
And through her fingers spy his manly face;
Sic signs as these, I trow, gang far to prove
That she was smitten with the pangs o' love.
"About that time I courted a bit lass,
And I was sair enamoured wi' her face.
I thought frae her if death would spare his dart,
I'd do my utmost to secure her heart;
When in love's coils I then designed to mention,
And lay before her my mature intention—
To fauld her to my breast, and then in course
To mak' her mine for better or for worse.
Ae day I spoke to John, just at the random,
That I would like to ha'e her memorandum;
He then forthwith took up his chalk and pencil,
And drew the face and outlines of my damsel;
I have it yet—but losh! I'm aff the track,
Ae day he went, 'twas lang ere he cam' back;
And when he came he couldna break his fast,
He look'd concerned and unco sair dooncast;
His mother coaxed him kindly to his bed,
But O! that night an unco life he led,
Poor lad! he raved, a fever had set in,
And sair afflicted were his kith and kin.

At length the night of darkness fled away,
The sun in triumph ushered in the day,
At middle day the fever ran its course,
And yet the lad was growing worse and worse,
His mother, then plied aff unto the toon,
Wi' anxious heart, to bring the doctor doon.
When comin' back alane, as sure's I'm born,
She saw John standin' by the muckle thorn;
She spoke, she cried, she screech'd wi' a' her might,
He glided off and vanished out o' sight!
She ferlied sair, she raised her eyes to heaven,
She prayed that a' her sins might be forgiven,
Aside the thorn she laid her bosom bare,
She prayed that God her only son would spare;
Her words re-echoed o'er the lonely lea—
'Oh! lift his load, and lay the load on me!'
When she got home, how sad it is to say,
His heart was still—his spirit gone away!
What tongue can tell the bitter scene of grief?
The tears of anguish could not bring relief.
Sorrow and sadness!—weary was the sigh—
The shrieks of anguish smote the very sky!"

JOHN A. BRUCE, ESQ., HAMILTON.

SIR:—

THE bound'ry line—the message cross'd it,
That you the marriage flag had hoisted,
Then wi' the news right hame I posted
Fu' gleg and gay,
And my ain winsome wife accosted
And thus did say:—

"Hurrah! John's gat a better-half,
Rin out and stick the auldest calf,
And cook it weel—I'll tak' my staff
And ca' our freens;
Guidfaith! we'll hae a hearty yaff
O'er beef and greens."

Then my guidwife did clasp a dirk,
And aff she sprang to do the wark,
And aff I scoured to Cameron, Clerk,
And Bruce McEwen,
And other friends, to taste the stirk
My wife was stewin'.

It just was chapin' four o'clock,
When at the door we heard a knock;
My guidwife ran to change her frock,
And ca' her daddie.
I turned the key; quo' I, "guid folk,
The dinner's ready!"

Sae down we sat to roast and stew,
We chewed the flesh and drank the broo,
And whan our kites were burstin' fu',
I ca'd the lasses,
"Bairns," quo' I, "we've gotten through,
Take aff the dishes."

Then frae her seat our Luckie bangs,
And to the press awa she gangs,
And brings the sugar and the tangs,
And glass and spoon,
Then wi' baith hands the grey-beard spangs,
And brings it doon.

Now when the toddy was approved,
And when the spirit in me moved,
Upon my shanks it me behoved,
To ca' a truce,
"Come, toast," quo' I, "ane lang I've lo'ed,
His name is Bruce."

I said, "we twa were thick thegether,
Our thoughts aye ran to ane another,
That Bruce to me was lang a brother
In word and deed;
To lose his friendship I wad rather
E'en lose my head!"

It struck the audience wi' amaze,
As forth I launched the word and phrase,
Man! how I yerkit up your praise—
My jaws did wallop
Just like a horse in cart or chaise
Whan at the gallop!

I tald them a' ye'd changed your life,
And to your breast had pressed a wife,
A lassie just as gleg's a knife,
And brisk an' bonnie,
Wha cam' frae 'bout the hills o' Fife
To mate wi' Johnie.

We drank your health wi' three times three,
Toasted the bride wi' glorious glee,
Then Cameron said, "aye let me see,"
(He spak' it fine),
"I hope their count o' bairns will be
Just twa times nine."

When we gat done wi' crack and jokin',
Wi' singin', snuffin' and pipe smokin',
And 'fore the party up was broken,
To cap the ploy,
I 'greed to send a written token,
And wish ye joy.

I hope when e'ening shuts her e'e,
When ye ha'e gat your drap o' tea,
Ye'll soon ha'e bairns on ilka knee,
And glower and smoke,
Or, wi' ae fit wi' cannie jee,
The cradle rock.

Ye'll then be quits wi' care and strife,
Ye'll feel the essence o' this life;
There sits your bonnie Scottish wife
Nae cares to cark,
Wi' needle, shears and ripping knife,
Mending your sark!

'Tis then the warld may birl aboot,
For it ye carena a sheep-cloot,
On ilk care ye plant your foot,
Nae griefs molest,
Ye'll let your pipe gang heedless out,
Syne slip to rest.

My Bruce! I pray for freedom's sake,
The Bruce's line will never brake,
Their hearts from right no power can shake,
No hand can turn;
The name that made the tyrant quake,
At Bannockburn.

I'm running out o' rhyme and clashes,
My muse is sometimes dour and fashous,
Although at times awa she dashes,
And no sae han'less;
Now, Sir, accept kind hearty wishes
Frae ANDREW WANLESS.

Who Should and Who Shouldn't.

Inscribed to John Bannerman, Esq.

IN days bygone, when tyrants held the rod,
The subject trembled at their very nod;
These days are changed—the manners growing worse,
Hirelings pay homage to the longest purse.

I know a man—a sage profoundly great,—
Who has for years contended against fate,
From morn to night, with willing heart and hand,
He'd strive to be "a something" in the land.
Free is his heart from black deceit and guile—
Vice has his frown and virtue has his smile.

In learned circles still he holds the sway,
And ticklish points can make as clear as day;
If doubters doubt, how quick upon the boards
He'll trip them up, and knock them down with words;
Yet no offense is found, he ne'er is slow
To pour the oil upon the fallen foe.

At evening's close, how oft with him I'd walk,
'Twas then I heard the majesty of talk;
On "this" he'd touch, on "that" he would descant,
His sounding words ne'er drivel'd into rant.
He'd take a pebble from the common ground,
And on it gaze and turn it round and round,
From small beginnings, clearly he would trace
Its age, its properties and race,
Proclaim it is volcanic in formation,
Then sum up all with pointed peroration.

The leaf upon the tree—the grassy plant,
With wisdom's aid, on these he can descant;
He knows a beetle from a creeping thing,
How reptiles bite and how the hornets sting,
The warbling birds that sing upon the sprey,
With cautious step he'd listen to their lay,
Or, stand in silence lest they'd fly away.

He e'en can show how nature's grand design
Has drawn 'tween species a dividing line;
Points out how Darwin in a wild delusion
Attempts to jumble all in a confusion;
Quizzes the "tail," denounces Darwin's plan,
Rejects his theory and condemns the man
Who digs in chaos, and forgets his God,
And sends his buncombe theories abroad!
How oft I've wished upon our evening walk,
Instead of me, that Darwin heard him talk.

The stars appear—the countless eyes of heaven;
He knows the pole—and well he knows the seven;
At this one points with a becoming gesture,
How it runs loose, and that one is a fixture.
At times he'll laugh and say some curious things,
Scout at the "tails," yet wish that he had wings
To fly through space and sweep through Saturn's rings,
And in his towering flight and trackless way,
Stop and pay homage to the god of day;
Then back to earth, to spend a space at home—
To take the pen and write a wond'rous tome!

When wars begin, how quickly he can trace
Who will be victor in the bloody race,
Denounces men who by the cannon stand,
And sweeps destruction o'er a wretched land,
Denounces men who fawn, and steal and fib,
And feed and fatten at the public crib.

Questions he settles, "yes," and sometimes "no,"
And say—" this statesman should do so and so;"
And in my ardor I have often said:
"This man has brains to be a nation's head!"
And yet this sage has fallen out of date,
He dines with want upon a pewter plate,
He stands behind the scenes—has grown gray,
And like a vision soon will pass away,
Or, like a light upon some distant coast,
That flickers—fades—then is forever lost!

* * * * * *

There lives a man, his name I need not tell,
For every town and village know him well,
He first appeared upon the public view,
To run an errand and to black a shoe;
Quick with his ear and ready with the talk,
He learned to swear, before he learned to walk;
Without a cap, or shoe upon his feet,
He'd toss the copper on the quiet street,
He'd lurk in barns or on door steps recline,
When pity spoke, how well the knave could whine,
With hungry throat gulph down compassions meal—
Laugh in his sleeve—then turn aside to steal.

Behind a fence, in some secluded yard,
He learned to deal and know the winning card,
He next began to swagger and to smoke,
To sing a song, and tell the silly joke.
One morn we missed him, and we did not mourn,
From his vile haunts the little imp was torn,—
To where the sinners have their ringlets shorn.

Some years had fled, and he came back once more,
Ten times more brazen than he was before;
One day I saw him standing in a crowd,
And while he stood, the knave was talking loud,
And as the laugh went round, he gave a wink,
And cried, " come, boys, and let us have a drink."

When next I saw him, how my eyes did stare,
I heard him talk and saw him beat the air—
"Elect me, friends!" the rest I did not hear,
I stood aside to shed the bitter tear.

He was elected! Vice aloud did crow—
And Virtue wept upon the couch of woe,
Yet, though the knave could neither read nor write,
With gilded hook he coaxed the crowd to bite;
What was the cause? the answer has no crook;
He gained his point with some one's pocket-book!

Who cannot catch the MORAL must be blind,
Hardened in heart—perverted in the mind,
The lesson may be learned from what I've said—
Reject the low and choose the higher grade,
Reject the vile who wear the brazen brand,
Elect the good and heaven will bless the land;
Choose men of worth—give wisdom power and place,
Then Faith and Hope will run an equal race!

TIB'S SLIGHTED ME, YE KEN.

Inscribed to A. McAdam, Esq.

E night I knocked at Tibby's door,
The dogs set up an unco roar,
Her mother loud the brutes did shoar,
As I gade snooling ben.

I speer'd if "Tibby wasna in?"
The auld wife's specks fell o'er her chin,
The auld man claw'd his cuits and shin,
And said he "didna ken."

He spak and speer'd where I cam frae,
And if I shank'd it a' the way;
She glower'd at me frae tap to tae,
But Tibby ne'er cam' ben.

I glanced aye at the but house door,
I heard a kissing skirling splore,
The sweat broke out at ilka pore,
Wha's there I'd like to ken ?

Wi' grief I scare could raise my head,
My heart felt like a lump o' lead,
I haflins prayed that I was dead,
Woes me! she ne'er cam' ben.

The auld man sair did glunch and gloom,
The wife wad neither sink or soom,
But aye she patter'd round the room,
Like an auld clockin' hen.

I sat and ga'e a kind o' grane,
My head and heart were cramm'd wi' pain,
Sae daised I scarce could rise my lane,
But Tibby ne'er cam ben.

At last, said I "I maun awa;"
The guidman ga'e his croon a claw,
The guidwife said, "guid guide us a',
Its on the stroke o' ten."

Then out I gade wi' hanging lugs,
'Mang grunts and granes and barking dowgs,
My heart strings ga'e sic rives and rugs,
I scarce could stand on en'.

As hame I gade amang the weet,
My head hang o'er twa shorking feet,
I envied lambs and sheep wha bleet,
And fend upon the fen.

Unmindfu' o' the guns and snares,
I envied e'en the maping hares,
The very brownies in their lairs—
Tib's slighted me ye ken.

The Wife and the Breeks.

Inscribed to John McCormick, Esq.

UPON an afternoon o' Monday,
I sat geck, geckin' at the winday;
Brightly the sun shone in the sky;
The smirkin' lasses trippit by,
The dogs about the street were friskin',
The lazy cows their tails were whiskin',
The bees were humming round the rose,
And gathering honey I suppose.
In-doors my ain respected wife
Seemed to renew her tak o' life:
E'en grannie laid aside her sadness,
And leugh wi' childish glee and gladness;
Aboot the floor our bairns were birlin',
And like to deave us wi' their skirlin';
And there I sat upon the Monday—
Geckin' and glowerin' out the winday.
Sudden the sky became o'ercast,
Hark! to the rumb'ling distant blast.
The cluds were gathering black and dour,
Here comes the swirlin' blindin' stoure.
"Grannie! by Jupiter the rain
Is splatterin' on the window pane;"
And as I sat, as quick as wink
Out door I saw a wife play jink;
In her right hand she stevely graspit
A muckle mouthed twa-handed basket.
Though quick she ran, I yet could trace
Grim desperation in her face.

Hark! grannie, to that thunder peel,
See! there's the wife at the claes reel.
Quick frae the lines the claes are whiskit,
Losh! how she bangs them in the basket.
As round and round the reel plays waddle,
Down comes the mutch, bed-gown and daidle.
How gleg she works, losh, wife, tak' heed,
Ye've gi'en that sark an unco screed,
Guid guide us a'! I'm bound to say
She's torn its very tail away.
Round goes the reel, the ropes are bare,
Except o' breeks a single pair;
She's waled the claes frae aff the cleeks,
But to the end she's left the breeks,
And by their bouk a child might scan
That they were made for her guidman;
There now, she's seized them by the legs,
Doon comes the breeks and wooden pegs,
Then quick as wink awa she gaes
And dashes them aboon the claes.
And why she left them to the end,
The deil o' me could comprehend!
Quo' grannie, "man, without a dou't,
She kens fu' weel what she's aboot;
An idiot could explain the matter—
She saved the breeks to kep the water."
"Grannie, I swear by my phylacterie,
Ye reason unco satisfactory;
Guidwife, what think ye 'bout the trews,
Do ye support your grannie's views?"
A mockriff rage in her I spied,
As she stood up and thus replied:
"Men's breeks I value no ae feather,
Sae dinna deave me wi' your blether."
She gained the door, and when she passed it,
Haith! she denounced baith breeks and basket,
Which plainly shows when men's at leisure,
Their wives are just a perfect treasure!

Now a' ye sages far and wide,
Wha on your hobby horses ride,
Wha cock your nose and look sae wise
Aboot the hidden mysteries,
Wha can explain, wi' great pretension,
Things far ayont our comprehension,
And kittle questions quick can solve,
How planets round the sun revolve,
Why light'nings flash and thunder rolls,
And how the earth aboot the polls
Turns round and round like a claes reel,
Or like an auld wife's spinnin' wheel.
My certy! they tell mair than that,
They say the warld's ends are flat,
If sae, guidfaith she's better manners,
Than lasses wha wear pads and panners.
E'en ministers, whan in the pu'pit,
Roar till their throats are dry and roupit;
The lives o' defunct Jews expoundin',
And godlessness with God confoundin';
Preaching 'bout men whose very name
Stands tapmaist on the rolls o' shame;
And what is curious and surprising,
For their black deeds apologizing!
Ye ministers, come, mend your manners,
And never mind the ancient sinners,
Come, try your eloquence and art,
Upon the living sinners heart;
So by your precept and example
Ye may convert a better sample:
A living dog, ye ken it's said,
Is better than a lion dead.
Yet, deil a ane o' ye can tell,
Nae better than I could mysel',
Why the guidwife upon the cleeks
Left to the last the guidman's breeks?
Which shows that men and geese may cackle,
And yet no just ken extra muckle!

JEAN AND DONALD;

OR, THE SMASHING OF THE TEA-POT.

A TRUE STORY.

Inscribed to Neil Taylor, Esq.

A number of people of the present generation, I have no doubt, can well remember the time when tea was considered a great rarity in Scotland, especially in the rural districts. Those who were in the habit of indulging in that beverage were looked upon by many as deluded mortals, and considered to be no better than the opium eater of our own period. In fact, the greater number of the inhabitants knew as little about tea as a cat knows about a snuff box. In corroboration of this, an old woman, called Tibby Gourlay, who lived in the parish of Westruther, one day fell very sick of an "onfa," for which no remedy could be obtained. The distressing news of Tibby's sickness reached the ears of the lady of Spottiswood, who immediately dispatched a servant with a quantity of tea to be administered to the invalid. The tea was tumbled into a porridge pot along with a quantity of water, and then boiled for a considerable time; the water was then thrown out of doors, and the leaves mashed up with butter, pepper and salt, and this mess was then served up to Tibby, who ate the whole with great energy and delight. Next morning, strange to tell, she was able to be up with the sun, and accomplished a heavy day's spinning on the big wheel to the satisfaction of herself and all concerned. She died about thirty years ago, aged ninety-nine. The following is written, not upon Tibby, but upon Jean and Donald, who were born and brought up in another part of the Heather Isle.

IN Islay's fine and fertile isle,
All in the county of Argyle,
There Donald lived, wha had a wife,
The dread and torment o' his life;
Afore he claimed Jean as his bride,
She e'en had traveled unco wide,
And learned to turn up her nose
At pease meal bannocks and at brose!
Ae year she winter'd 'bout Dunbarton,
And tied her stockin' wi' a garten;
She even tried hard to get married,
But a' her purposes miscarried;
She had no friends about Alaska,
But had an aunt wha lived in Glasgow,
Sae faith, she mounted on a coach,
And to that city she did hotch,
When there she fell in deep dejection,
For she had lost her aunt's direction,
She speered at folk and bairns in plenty,
If they ken'd aught aboot her aunty?
At last by kind o' luck or fate,
She faund her in the Gallowgate.
Her aunty was a lonely woman,
She didna ken her niece was comin';
She gave a jump—she stood amazed
When on the stranger's form she gazed!
Then both did raise an Islay yell,
When in ilk other's arm they fell!
Then Jean exclaimed, "my woe is past,
I've found my aunty at the last."

How nice it is on some occasions,
To meet with one's own blood relations,
But sweeter far 'tis to the lover,
To meet and kiss and hug the other;
High is that love, 'tis oft hysteric,
And far above my panegyric.

O ! love, fain would I thee extol—
The prop and centre of the soul !

The aunt then said, "my darling niece,
In size ye've made a great increase,
'Tis only twenty years by-gane
Ye couldna stand your leefu' lane !
Guidfaith ! ye're now a winsome straper
As ever gaed in gown or wrapper,
My certy ! ye're as fine a lass
As e'er keek'd in a looking glass ;
Gang down the stair, my niece, so dear,
And bring me up a jug o' beer,
A drop o' beer in glass or measure,
Will calm my heart that loups wi' pleasure,
And after that, 'tween you and me,
I'll mask a hair o' guid black tea."
These words were barely out her lips,
When down the stairs Miss Jeanie trips,
And brings her aunty up a jug
O' beer filled to the very lug ;
Sae soon as they the liquor tasted,
Their tongues for no a minit rested.

When aunty gat the tea things ready,
Miss Jean sat down just like my lady,
And aye she took the other sup,
Then raised her neb up frae the cup—
Twisting her head—see there, look at her,
Just like a hen whan drinking water ;
Her aunt gecked at her with affection,
Jean thought hersel' complete perfection !

'Tis strange that poor deluded craters
Will ape the manners o' their betters,
And turn and twist, and put on airs,
Like horses at the country fairs !
'Tis a disease bred in the bone,
It rages rife frae zone to zone,

Wi' this e'en Hornie was diseased,
Whan frae the heaven's he was heezed,
But faith, another sang he routit,
Whan 'mang the brimstone he was coupit!
Folk! folk, I pray, tak' my example,
And no in Satan's footsteps trample,
The bard wi' kicks frae fortune's foot,
Has gat his pride clean knockit out,
If ony's left, whan a' is dune,
It wadna lade a mustard spoon!

Whan at their tea, midst joke and crack,
The auld aunt's mind gade wand'ring back
To times whan she did hear the roar
O' billows lashing Islay's shore!
Then she inquired "if ducks and drakes
Aye swam about the coves and lakes;
And if the fowls in pairs and flocks
Still bred amang the muckle rocks;
And if Neil Taylor still gangs out
To blister horses, dogs and nowte;
And if his wife, and bairnies monie,
Are a' as guid as they are bonnie;
If Duncan Campbell blythe was singin',
And to the island still was hingin',
And if his thirty-second cousin
Had now o' weans a baker's dizen?"
To a' these questions, and far mair,
Miss Jean made answer on the square.

For sax lang weeks the twa were bousin',
Baith night and day they were carousin';
At length whan tea and toast gat scanty,
Miss Jean did say unto her aunty:
"I trow I'll gang the road I came,
I'm grienin' sairly to gang hame,
I've gi'en ye now a guid lang ca',
I'm sure it's time I was awa."

The twa shook hands, then aff Jean flounced,
And down her grannie's stair she pounced,
She darted for the Broomielaw,
Whan she gat there how she did blaw :
It was nae lang ere down the Clyde,
Wi' Jean on board, a ship did glide.

Sweet stream ! O, may thou aye meander,
On earth there is nae river grander !
By thee a bonnie lass I courted,
Wi' my fond heart she played and sported ;
My lovely, fair-haired, blooming Susan
Did prove to be a mere delusion !
I'd sing o' Clyde with livelier glee
If Susan hadna slighted me ;
False maid ! she shot a cruel dart
That still is stickin' in my heart !
Both night and day I have a doubt
That time will never drag it out.

Now twenty hours it took, or more,
To land Miss Jean on Islay's shore ;
As Donald stood upon the key
His future wife he chanced to see,
Though he was unco short o' sight,
He saw her frae the ship alight.
She hadna been on shore a week,
Till he on her again did keek,
Then o'er the lugs in love he sluced
Sae soon as he was introduced.

Arouse, my muse ! spread wide your wing,
'Bout Donald and his darling sing,
His love was not an idle dream,
'Twas higher than the rainbow's rim,
Yes, Donald's love, before he wed,
Was deeper than the oceans bed !
'Twas brighter than an infant's eye,
And fairer than the summer's sky :
Jean's heart was like a stream run dry.

How Jean did giggle, smile and smirk,
When she led Donald to the kirk,
And when the nuptial knot was tied
Wi' love poor Donald shook and sighed,
But Jean did stand, the graceless limmer,
Thinking 'bout nothing but her dinner!
When they gat hame to marriage feast,
I needna say Jean did her best,
She tried the pork, the beef and ham,
Pig's feet, hen's legs and roasted lamb;
But for the haddies and the herrin'
She said she wasna' muckle carein',
Then she devoured as a desert
A moderate share o' tea and tart.

Ten years flew by o' married life—
Ten years o' badg'ring, bick'ring strife;
Love out their door slink'd aff wi' passion,
As care and hardship took possession!
Poor Donald gat as lean's a craw,
And ilka day away did fa',
He just was perfect skin and bane,
Yet still, he ne'er complained o' pain.
Though want was in poor Donald's spoon,
Jean's face was like the rising moon!
She managed weel, in spite o' fate,
To aye hae plenty on her plate,
She turned a kind o' tousy drab,
And thought 'bout nothing but her gab!

It fell upon an afternoon
Whan Donald's wark was early done,
As he was cannie slinkin' hame,
He thought he'd cheat his sturdy dame,
And buy a half a pound o' butter,
And ha'e a kind o' secret supper;
He gained his door and in his garret
He creepit like an evil spirit,

He glow'red about—his wife was missin'
He thought that was a heaven's blessin',
Then frae the press he took a platter
And on it slaster'd a' the butter,
Then set it down upon the dresser.

When rinnin' out to get some meal
He ran against daft Rab McNeil;
"Gang in," he said, "I'll soon be back,
Syne Rabbie, we will ha'e a crack."
Poor Donald felt a wee contented,
As things were working as he wanted.
Now ben the house daft Rabbie goes—
He saw the butter 'fore his nose,
And then the poor misguided lad
Did hide it underneath the bed!
Back Donald cam', wi' strange surprise,
He scarcely could believe his eyes,
He glow'red, he gave a dismal groan—
Then roared, "where is the butter gone?"
Now Rab did on his cantle clat,
"The thief," he said, "must be the cat."
Then Donald swore unto his frien',
If on the brute he'd clap his e'en,
He'd wring her neck just like a craw,
And dash her head against the wa',
He'd gi'e her sic a fearfu' blatter,
She ne'er again wad steal his butter!
"For that," quo' Rab, "ye needna grane—
See! there she sits on the jamb stane!"
Then Donald whispers, "Rab, be quick,
And rax me ower that muckle stick,
And I will gi'e her sic a billet
Will mak' her life flee up her gullet!"

As Rabbie handed ower the rung,
Grim silence sat on Donald's tongue,
His mouth and e'en were open wide,
As on his tiptoes he did glide,

He raised the rung aboon his croon,
Wi' fearfu' yerk the rung cam' doon!
A something ga'e a crack—a crash—
A something on his face played splash;
Then Donald yelled, "I'm dead! I'm gone!
I'm burning to the very bone!
Cat's blood is just as hot as fire,
Oh! Rabbie, come, till I expire!"
Then Rabbie roared, "Ye've missed the cat
And smashed to atoms the tea-pat!"
Then Donald howled, "the deil tak' me,
I never kent Jean swallow'd tea,
I ken it now, and here I swear it,
Henceforth she'll never drink na mair o't,
I'll put an end to her extortion,
For death this night will be her portion!
This night I'll mak' her change her pasture,
My faith! but she's a fine tea waster;
She'll live on tea and finely fare,
While I maun gang, I do declare,
Just like a wraith aboon the grund,
And live on brose and heaven's wind!
Her black misdeeds ha'e now nae clock,
She's let her cat clean out the poke!"
As Donald ended this harangue,
His wife into the house played bang,
And as the twa began to roar,
Prudence step'd up and shut the door.

EPITAPH.

Donald is gane—his cares are o'er—
He sleeps on Islay's fertile shore,
Cats he'll ne'er mistake again
For teapots standin' on jamb stane,
Nae butter he needs in his brose,
His sad career is at a close!
And Jean, his wife, now lies at rest
Upon his cold and lifeless breast.

A Weak Man and a Strong Woman.

Inscribed to C. Tyner, Esq., Hamilton, Ont., an unco auld friend.

WE met beneath the trysting tree,
The light o' love was in her e'e,
I knew her love was a' for me,
That Peggy would be mine.

We wander'd o'er the flow'ry brae,
To where the rippling waters play,
I kissed her lips, she ne'er said nay,
I thought she was divine.

I saw the blush upon her cheek,
I heard her words sae mild and meek,
Wi' joy I scarce could stand or speak,
Such love there was lang-syne.

Soon we were wed, what next befell
I think black burning shame to tell,
For soon her tongue went like a bell,
With grief sair I did pine.

She aften swinged me aff my chair,
She filled my heart with black despair,
And loaded me wi' tons o' care,
As ye may well opine.

If she had yatter'd wi' her tongue,
And been less free to use the rung,
To her, through life, I might ha'e clung,
And thought my lot was fine.

I've heard some wives when things went 'rang,
Would whistle up, or sing a sang,
But Peg, wi' rage, my throat would spang—
Afore I counted nine.

I'll saddle up my pacing horse,
And heckle her wi' a divorce;
Then she may live with black remorse—
She'll never more be mine.

By night and day, I'll seek a wife
Who will bring comfort to my life,
We'll feast on love and fast from strife—
And aye with Cupid dine.

But Peg saw me girth up my steed,
Slap-dash she came with headlang speed!
And like a vice she held my head
And grasped the halter line!

She cried, "ye sumph, gang in the house,"
I sleekit in just like a mouse,
Hech me! I didna craw sae crouse,
But sore did fidge and whine.

I thought it best to bow and bend,
And think upon my latter end,
For Oh! she gave me such a send
As nearly broke my spine.

"Oh! Peg," I yelled, "take in the horse,
I ne'er will ride for a divorce,
Have mercy, or ye'll end my course—
Wi' that lang halter line."

As Tam ga'e the last sentence vent,
Instanter, Peg did sair repent,
To hug and kiss they briskly went,
Fu' canty and fu' fine.

Now ilka man, baith far and near,
Just gi'e your wife your breeks to wear,
And let her still the helm steer,
As Adam did lang syne.

Your life will be a honeymoon,
If ye just coax her into tune,
And feed her wi' a soothing spoon—
And swear she is divine!

A Reformation.

Inscribed to Wylie Nielson, Esq.

UPON a cold and rainy night,
When moon and stars were out of sight,
A-coming down the lonely street,
A little child I chanced to meet;
The wee bit lassie's feet were bare,
The rain had droukit a' her hair,
And as the child came running near,
I trow her heart was filled wi' fear;
A something whisper'd me to stand,
I took her kindly by the hand,
Then said, "my child, what is amiss,
To bring ye out a night like this?"
The lassie hung her head wi' shame,
Then said, "Oh! sir, come to our hame;"
I strok'd the bonnie bairnies hair,
I carried her wi' cannie care;
The rain in torrents still did pour
As we twa reached her father's door.
Within the house I heard a moan—
A shriek—a wild unearthly groan;
I saw a sight—a man was there
Sunk in the depths of black despair,
His bloodshot eyes were staring wild,
Anon he wept just like a child,
And then with terror loud did yell,
Contending with an inward hell,

Then on the ground he down would lie
To wrestle with his agony!
He trembling crouch'd with fear and dread,
The demons hovered round his head,
He prayed, he cried on bended knee—
"O God, have mercy upon me!"
I said, "may heaven hear the prayer,
And calm the bosom of despair."
The little child, Oh! how she wept,
As to her father's side she cript,
He clasped her to his frenzied breast,
And tenderly her lips he pressed;
And as the tears fell down like rain,
He cried, "no drink I'll touch again!"
His "ministering angel" came,
He called her kindly by her name,
Then said, "from drink I stop this night,
Henceforth I'll be a Rechabite."

He kept his word, contentment reigns,
He broke the drunkard's galling chains,
Now peace and plenty smile once more,
And poverty has left his door.

Join, brothers, then with heart and hand,
The seed of Hope sow in the land,
And strive with all your might to save
The drunkard from the drunkard's grave.

A Scotch Sangster's Comin'.

Inscribed to T. McGregor, Esq., President of St. Andrew's Society, Detroit.

ON Monday, in St. Andrew's Ha'
Rally! men and brithers a',
Send the news baith far and near—
A Scottish Sangster's comin' here!
Deck'd fu' braw in Highland kilt,
He will sing us monie a lilt
'Bout auld Scotland's heath'ry hills,
Birken glens and wimplin' rills,
Where the lav'rocks sweetly sing,
Where the bonnie blue bells spring.
Hame! we'll ne'er forget ava
'Till our latest breath we draw.

While the daisy decks the lea,
Scotia's sangs will never dee—
Floating down time's silent river,
Time and they will die together;
Send the news baith far and near,
A Scottish Sangster's comin' here!
Nane like him our sangs can han'le—
He's the lad to haud the can'le;
Sangs o' Scotland he will sing,
Will make the very rafters ring;
Sangs o' dule and dark despair,
Will mak' us rug and rive our hair,
Sangs wi' monie a weary mane,
Wad melt a very heart o' stane;

Sangs o' love, o' joy, and fear,
Heartfelt words forever dear.

Come ye lasses blythe and braw,
Welcome to St. Andrew's ha' !
His funny cracks will mak' for weeks
The tears rin down your bonnie cheeks,
Folk ! ye manna stay at hame,
That wad be a burnin' shame—
Send the news baith far and near,
A Scottish Sangster's comin' here.

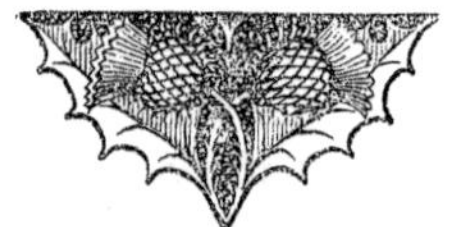

GRAIGIE CASTLE.

AIR—*Catherine Ogie.*

Upon a rocky bank of the clear winding Dye, in a beautiful and secluded dell, the ruins of Craigie Castle can still be seen. Some years ago, it was a favorite amusement of the school boys to hurl the stones of this ruin down the deep declivity, and with something akin to awe, watch them, as they rolled, dashed and plunged into the pool below. A little to the right of this ruin is Peel Hill, where a fine view of the surrounding district can be obtained. From its name there can be no doubt, that upon its top the beacon fire has often been kindled to warn the inhabitants that danger was near—that the enemy was approaching. There is every evidence to show that the Lammermoors, being so near the Scotch and English borders, must have been the scene of many a deadly conflict. There is a tradition that the Dye received its name from its being literally dyed with the blood of the slain. To the west of Peel Hill is a place called Main-Slaughter-law, where the turf and peat diggers have frequently turned up the implements of warfare.

In this vicinity, also, there is an Otterburn, and the writer in the "Statistical Account of Scotland" surmises that this may have been the ground where the celebrated battle of that name took place. Some miles distant, upon a high elevation, stand the Twin-law Cairns, regarding which, tradition has it, that in view of the two armies of the Picts and Scots a deadly conflict took place between twin brothers. One of the brothers had been stolen in his infancy by the Picts, and as the two fell to rise no more an aged warrior made known their relationship. Tradition also says that the soldiers of both armies formed a line of some miles in extent and handed stones from one to another from the bed of the stream of Watch to build the Cairns, which remain to this day. Regarding this tradition, the Rev. Dr. Jamieson, of Westruther, published in the work before mentioned a beautiful ballad that escaped the researches of Sir Walter Scott, while compiling his "Minstrelsy of the Scottish Border," and which the reverend gentleman wrote down from the recital of two old men, who resided in that locality.

The following ballad is founded on a tradition that the lord of the castle before mentioned had gone to the wars, and left his young wife to mourn his absence for "twice seven long months" and that on a moonlight night she heard the drum beat. She ran to the turret of the castle overlooking the Dye, and while there she observed her lord make a dangerous leap across the stream at a place called the "Darin-step," and from this cause it is said, her strength forsook her, and the child she held in her arms fell into the abyss below. The ballad tells the rest.

THE sun had set ayont the hill,
The moon on high was creeping,
When on her couch a lady fair
Wi' sorrow sair was weeping;
And aye she wrung her milk-white hands,
And frae her e'en sae bonny
The waefu' tears ran rowin' doon,
Unseen, unkent by ony.

Her lord was e'en as brave a knight
  As e'er wore kilt or pladie;
Now he has gone unto the wars
  And left his winsome lady.
He bade farewell unto his bride,
  He kissed her lips sae bonny,
He's kissed her ower and ower again,
  She's gi'en him kisses monie.

Now he has buckled on his sword,
  His gallant steed is ready;
The waesome tears fell ower his cheek
  When parting frae his lady.
Twice seven lang months had fled away;
  Her wounded heart was breakin',
For still the thought wad come and go—
  That she was left forsaken.

And aye she wrung her lily hands
  Upon the bed of sorrow,
And sair she longed again to see
  The dawin' o' the morrow.
She clasp'd her infant to her breast,
  She heard the distant drumming,
Wi' joy she climbed the turret high
  To watch her true knight coming.

She saw him leap the Darin-step,
  Wi' dread her heart did shiver,
Then frae her arms the child fell down—
  Down in the raging river!
The heavens heard her shriek of woe,
  The warrior saw his lady
Leap from the castle's dizzy hight,
  In death she clasp'd her baby!

Her Heart was all Mine Own.

Air—*Gloomy Winter's now awa.*

GLOOMY days and weary nights,
  Sad and lonely I am now,
Grief is monarch of my heart,
  Sorrow sits upon my brow.
In the spring-time of my life,
  I woo'd a maiden fair to see,
In the summer of my life—
  Death has ta'en my love from me.

O'er the by-gone path of time,
  O'er the joy and o'er the care,
O'er the tear and o'er the smile,
  Mem'ry lingers here and there.
Her eye was like the morning bright
  When the mists away have flown,
Her lips were like the budding rose,
  And her heart was all mine own.

O'er her dark and lonesome grave
  Birds may sing and flowers may bloom,
Nature may with joy rejoice,
  But my heart is in the tomb.
By her heart forever still,
  By her eyes in darkness set,
Till I draw my latest breath,
  My Mary I will ne'er forget!

Belle Isle Aboon Detroit.

Air—*Logan Braes.*

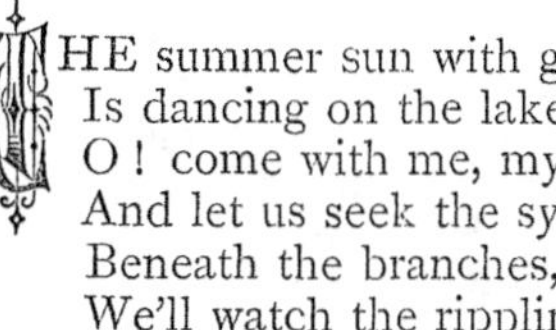

HE summer sun with golden beam
Is dancing on the lake and stream;
O! come with me, my lovely maid,
And let us seek the sylvan glade.
Beneath the branches, spreading wide,
We'll watch the rippling waters glide;
Come! let us see the wild rose smile—
Upon the banks of sweet Belle Isle.

With mellow note the blue-bird sings,
How lovely there the violet springs!
And there the honeysuckles twine,
'Mang scented groves of eglantine.
I'll pull the lilacs fresh and fair,
And twine them in your golden hair;
While love will all our cares beguile—
Amang the groves of sweet Belle Isle.

We'll wander through the woodland green,
And linger by each fairy scene;
Though nature's face be fair to see—
My heart will fondly dwell on thee!
I'll gaze upon thine eyes so blue,
Our vows of love we will renew—
And Truth will speak, and Hope will smile
Amang the groves of sweet Belle Isle.

My Love, O! Come to Me.

Air—*Banks o' Doon.*

WHEN vict'ry sheath'd the sword of strife,
And gentle peace once more did reign,
With feeble step, and weary heart,
A soldier sought his home again.
He stood beside a lonely grave,
And o'er his cheek the tears did flow—
His throbbing heart was like to break
For her who sleeps in death below!

In life her heart to him was true,
In thought, in word—with latest breath
She cried, "my love, O! come to me,"
Then sank into the arms of death!
On battlefield, in danger's hour,
The soldier never feared the foe,
But now his heart is like to break—
For her who sleeps in death below!

He kneel'd upon the lonely grave,
He kissed the cold and lifeless clay,
He linger'd long—then left the spot,
The hand of anguish led the way.
Thus onward to the weary end,
The bitter tears of grief will flow,
The soldier's heart is in the grave
With her who sleeps in death below.

Detroit is the Town for Me.

Air—*Willie was a Wanton Wag.*

THE river sweeps by Sarnia bank,
Then glides alang sae merrilye,
The lilies smile upon Stag Isle—
And violets blush sae bonnilye.
The roses smile upon Belle Isle,
The birds sing sweet upon the tree,
Though lasses fair dwell in St. Clair,
Detroit is the town for me!

The pine trees wave on Huron's shore
The clover blooms on Moretown lea,
At Algonac men fondly talk,
And court the lasses gallantlye,
On Fromville brae the lammies play,
In Walpole woods the robins flee,
Though lasses fair dwell in St. Clair,
Detroit is the town for me!

Detroit river saftly glide,
Ye birds sing love on ilka tree,
Sing to my love in bush and grove,
Your richest sweetest melody,
Sing to my love your blythest songs,
And fill her gentle heart wi' glee,
Though lasses fair dwell in St. Clair,
Detroit is the town for me!

Jeanie Bell.

Air—*O' a' the airts the winds can blaw.*

LASSIE cam' unto our toon
   Whan flow'rs were blooming fair;
'Mang a' the bonnie blushing flow'rs,
   Nane wi' her could compare.
The rose-bud in the dewy morn
   Smiles sweetly in the dell,
But sweeter far the rosy lips
   O' bonnie Jeanie Bell.

She has sae monie winsome ways,
   Sae modest, kind and true,
A perfect heaven's reflected in
   Her eyes sae bonnie blue.
The birds that sing in green-wood shaw
   In sangs their love may tell,
But words can never speak the love
   I ha'e for Jeanie Bell!

May a' that's guid aye guide her steps
   Alang life's thorny way,
May ilka year in a' her life,
   Be a'e lang summer's day.
Oh! Jeanie dinna leave our toon,
   I ne'er can say "farewell,"
But stay and be a joy to me,
   My bonnie Jeanie Bell!

Jineral O'Neil.

Air—*Johnnie Cope,*

EIL sint a letther from New York,
Sayin', "Meself will show yees bloody work,
Kanucks I'll cut yees up like pork,
Whin I meet yees in the marnin'!"

Och! Jineral O'Neil are yees spakin' yet?
Or are the Kanucks quakin' yet?
If yees be spakin' meself will wait,
To advance on Malone in the marnin'.

Whin John Bull looked the letther upon,
Shure he began to rout and groan,
"Kanucks," he cried, "Neil's at Malone,
We'll fight him in the marnin'."
Och! Jineral O'Neil, etc.

Now Jineral be as thrue as steel,
It's yoursilf will make the Kanucks squeel,
It's yoursilf will give thim a hot pill
Ave shot an' shell in the marnin'.
Och! Jineral O'Neil, etc.

Whin O'Neil did hear the Kanuck John
Wad be afther fighting at Malone,
He got a dray to jump upon—
To vamose away in the marnin'."
Och! Jineral O'Neil, etc.

Faith now O'Neil it was not fair
To draw yer sword and bloody spear,
An' thin to run just like a deer—
Away from the Bull in the marnin'.
Och! Jineral O'Neill, etc.

Whin Jineral O'Neil to the station came,
He swore his stomach was to blame,
"Be the powers the wind's got in my wame,
It blows right cowld this marnin'."
Och! Jineral O'Neil, etc.

Whin in the jail, the brave O'Neil
Began to yell just like a diel,
"Bedad!" he cried, "a snake or eel
Is down me throat this marnin'."
Och! Jineral O'Neil, etc.

"Och! if St. Patrick would arise,
This sarpint banish—blast me eyes,
I'd mince the Kanucks up in pies
An' eat thim all in the marnin'."
Och! Jineral O'Neil, etc.

The Bull thin raised his tail on high,
An' gave a rout that shook the sky,
Thin Neil began to pipe his eye,
An' shake wid the ague in the marnin'.
Och! Jineral O'neil, etc.

Shure now O'Neil it was not fair,
Upon the line to rip and tare,
An' thin to flee, the L—d knows where—
An' leave yer men in the marnin'!
Och! Jineral O'Neil, etc.

The Men o' the Merse.

Air—*Laird o' Cockpen.*

Inscribed to W. Stevenson, Esq., Dunse, Scotland.

WHERE the Watch and the Dye and the Whitadder
rins
Doon to the Tweed where auld England begins;
There lived the heroes, that whither or no,
Wad fight for their country and lounder the foe.
In the front o' the battle, sae gallant and true,
The Merse Men where there wi' their bonnets o' blue;
The tyrants we read o' in prose and in verse,
Ne'er wanted *twa strokes* frae the Men o' the Merse.

The Men o' the Border! no tyrant could scare,
They ne'er run awa though the Percy was there,
When Liberty trembled, they never knew fear,
They aye did their best wi' the sword and the spear.
The Men o' the Border! auld England kens weel,
Are made o' guid stuff frae the head to the heel,
At the war cry, "A Douglas!" the foe would disperse,
In terror they'd flee frae the Men o' the Merse.

How sweet are the haughs and the glens o' the Forth!
How grand and majestic the hills o' the North!
The Clansmen may brag o' their big Lochnagar,
But our bonnie Tweedside is sweeter by far.
Our lasses are sweet as the rose o' the bower,
Ye'll no find their match in the warld out-ower,
And men wha in English or Gallic converse,
Maun a' knuckle doon to the Men o' the Merse!

THE BANKS O' THE DYE,

AIR—*Banks o' the Devon.*

THE sun o' the summer had set by the mountain,
And the gold clouds o' gloamin' were fading away;
And the sigh of the winds, 'mang the broom and the breckan,
Were humming a dirge o'er the fa' o' the day.
The moon had arisen sae pale and sae pensive,
And the twinkling stars shone bright in the sky;
How waesome my thoughts, and how weary I wander'd
Alane by the banks o' the clear winding Dye.

The hazels were bending a-down in the streamlet,
Their tassels wav'd meek in the moon's silv'ry beam;
And the cliffs of the rocks hung silent and dreary,
As if wafted to sleep by the lull of the stream.
The Dye ran sae dowie, that ance ran sae cheerie;
How dreary she murmurs by bank and by brae;
The flow'rs and the daisies wi' dew-drops are weeping,
There's naething looks gladsome since Mary's away.

How weary I wander, how sadly I linger,
Each wave of thy stream speaks of her that is gone;
Each sigh of the winds, as they ripple thy bosom,
Brings a tear for the joys that forever are flown.
No more can these joys again gladden my bosom,
For now I am friendless, forsaken and lone;
My heart no more throbs with enraptur'd emotion,
Since Mary, my Mary, forever is gone!

BONNIE NELL.

AIR—"*There was a lass and she was fair.*

HOW clearly rins the stream o' Watch,
By monie a brae and broomy dell,
It's howes and knowes nae stream can match,
By it I lo'ed my bonnie Nell.

O! Nellie I did lo'e thee weel,
There's no a heart could lo'e thee mair;
At mirkest hour to thee I'd steal,
Thou wert mine a' mine only care.

But now I gang a' wae and lane;
My Nellie's frae me ta'en awa,
I'll never see my love again,
My heart has now nae joy ava.

O Watch! how clearly rins thy stream,
By monie a brae and broomy dell,
By thee I dreamed life's fondest dream,
I woo'd, to tine, my bonnie Nell.

THE LANG TAILOR O' WHITBY.

AIR—*Laird o' Cockpen.*

THE lang tailor o' Whitby gaed doon to Port Hope,
And he ca'd at an inn, and he rang for a chop.
He drank a' the day; then the lang tailor said:
"Light a lamp, Mr. Landlord, and show me to bed."

Next morning, the tailor trip'd light down the stair,
"Ho! landlord," said he, "perhaps you're aware
That money is tight. I must go by the cars,
And instead of the dollars take two pair of drawers!"

Then the landlord replied, "these are just what I need,"
Then the tailor went off with respectable speed;
In a half hour or more the landlord up crept,
And he looked in the room where the tailor had slept.

He gazed at the bed; then sank down on a chair,
And he swat and he swore, and he tore at his hair,
His *twa* sheets were made into *twa* pair o' drawers,
And the tailor o' Whitby was off with the cars!

THE COW AVE CHICAGO.

AIR—*Irish Washerwoman.*

MRS. Leary O'Leary lived west in Chicago,
One night she did make both her tongue an' her jaw go,
"Bedad!" she says, "Pat, be aff wid yees now,
An' be afther the milk of our iligent cow!"
Thin Patsy did say, "may the divil reject us,
An' the howly St. Patrick forever protect us;"
He thin seized the pail and the kerosene lamp,
An' aff to the barn like a hero did tramp.

The barn-door whin he reach'd, he gave a loud bawl,
Then Pat danced a jig wid the cow in the stall;
He caught the cow's tail an' he made her leap round—
Thin the kerosene lamp he set down on the ground.
It stood purty an' bright 'mong the straw and the hay,
Thin Pat took the pail and wint milking away;
Sure he sang an' he whistled, an' swore at his mother,
As he filled up the pail an' emptied the udder.

Thin the leg ave the cow was seized wid the cramp,
Sure she straightened it out 'gainst the kerosene lamp;
Just as Patsy's mamma to her hammock wint sighing—
Sure her iligent cow an' her Patsy were frying.
Whin the fire an' the flames wint raging an' roaring,
Bad luck! Mrs. Leary wint sleeping and snoreing;
Whin she woke, faith, she made both her tongue and
her jaw go,
Troth! she swore that her cow ne'er set fire to Chicago!

LITTLE NELLIE.

AIR—*Roys' Wife.*

NELLIE is the sweetest lassie
E'er I saw atween the een,
She can lilt and sing sae bonnie—
O! she is a cantie queen!
I wadna gi'e my bonnie bairnie
For a' the gear that ye can name,
If I tint my toddlin' dawtie,
Mine wad be a dowie hame!

There she's runnin' round the housie,
Just as crouse as crouse can be,
See, she's playin' wi' the pussie,
Now she's dancing on my knee.
Haud awa, ye little hempie,
Touts! my cantle's unco bare,
Time and you are just twa randies,
Pouin' out my pickle hair.

Now she's ta'en aff shoe and stockin'
  Round about the floor to creep,
In her chair, wi' glee, she's rockin';
  Losh! the bairn is gaun to sleep.
Come to me, my bonnie hinnie—
  Ye're the pink o' a' the toon,
May the wale o' heaven's blessings
  Aye upon my pet fa' doon.

Cut the strings—tak' out the buttons;
  Losh! she's sleepin' like a tap;
Hushy bushy bonnie dawtie,
  Lift her cannie aff my lap.
In her cradle saftly lay her,
  Hushy bushy baby loo,
Sweetly sleep my wee bit totum—
  Angels guard my wee bit doo!

Her Love for Me did Wither.

Air—*Coming through the Rye.*

OH! my heart is wae and weary,
  Sad as sad can be,
Anna vowed to be my dearie,
  Anna's slighted me.
Oft we sat beside the fountain
  Where the lilies spring,
Oft we lingered by the mountain
  Where the linties sing.

Then, the daisy smiled so meekly—
  To the violet blue,
Then, the lark did sing sae sweetly,
  When my love was true.

Oft we wand'red through the meadow
  In the starry hours,
Fondly I would watch her shadow,
  Kiss the dewy flowers.

When the autumn winds were sighing
  O'er the lonely lea,
When the drooping flow'rs were dying—
  Sorrow came to me,
Hoping she was constant ever—
  Hope gave way to grief;
Alas! her love for me did wither
  Like the autumn leaf.

Come, Sweetheart, Come.

Air—*I Think of Thee.*

WINTER is gone and the west winds are blowing,
  Down the hill-side the clear stream is flowing,
  On bank and on brae primroses are springing,
  And up in the lift the lavrocks are singing.
The breeze on the pool is rippling and sleeping,
Up on the pine-tree the ivies are creeping,
Down in the glen grow the cowslip and gowan,
And high on the bank wave the ash-tree and rowan.

Come! sweetheart, come! let us go by the rushes,
Down where the birds sing amang the green bushes!
The blackbird will warble so blithesome and cheerie,
The linnet a love song will sing to my dearie.
There's a spot in th' dell where th' limpid stream gushes,
Where the rose, like your cheek, is blooming with blushes,
Where the silv'ry willows like ringlets are flowing,
And the sunbeams are dancing, and coming and going.

There, while the ring-doves are cooing above thee,
I'll tell thee, my sweetheart! how dearly I love thee;
There, while we wander 'mang gowans and daisies,
The whispering echo will hear of your graces.
Then Truth will rejoice—our vows will not die, love,
The lark on the gold-cloud will waft them on high, love,
Come! sweetheart, come! let us go by the rushes,
Down where the birds sing amang the green bushes.

WHO'S COMIN'?

AIR—*Donald Caird.*

MR. PETER Fraser's comin',
Blaw the pipes and set them bummin',
Till ilka man and ilka woman
Ken that Peter Fraser's comin';
Tell ilka man and ilka woman
That hurdle-louping Peter's comin'.

Wi' little fyke and little labor
He's the lad can toss the caber—
Toss it here and toss it there,
Toss it to the deil kens where;
Tell ilka man and ilka woman
That caber-tossing Peter's comin'.

Donald Dinnie at a race
Is nothing but a big disgrace,
The very spirits in the air—
Cry, "Donald dinna rin nae mair:"
Tell ilka man and ilka woman
That running Peter Fraser's comin'.

Donald's back can scarcely bend—
He's like a sack set up on end,
Or like a broken auld bass fiddle
Wi' a string tied round its middle :
    Tell ilka man and ilka woman
    That bounding Peter Fraser's comin'.

It's a sight to see him rinnin',
He's the lad can wax McLennan,
Gives a spring and off he flies—
Like an arrow through the skies :
    Tell ilka man and ilka woman
    That springing Peter Fraser's comin'.

Not a man can run like Peter,
At a loup he is a leaper,
At a toss he is a tosser :—
The muse has fled—nae man can boss her,
Notwithstanding Fraser's comin'.
    Tell ilka man and ilka woman
    That louping Peter Fraser's comin'.

Kate o' Boontree.

Air—*Bonnie Dundee.*

SWEET Kate o' Boontree, ye maun a' understand,
Has a dark rolling e'e and a lily-white hand ;
My certy ! she's played unco havoc wi' me,
I'm fairly bewitched wi' sweet Kate o' Boontree.

I think o' her beauty, perfection and grace,
And I dream o' her ringlets, her ribbons and lace ;
Though absent, guidfaith ! she's aye present wi' me,
In the heart o' my bosom dwells Kate o' Boontree !

'Twas no lang ago I thought love was a joke,
But now my heart loups like a cat in a poke;
Ilka hair on my head I would willingly gi'e
For twa or three kisses frae Kate o' Boontree.

Afore I saw Kate, I am free to declare,
I whistled and sang like a lark in the air,
But now in my bonnet I've gotten a bee,
That hums a' the day about Kate o' Boontree.

At times I will stand and forget mysel' sair,
Then doon I will plump on a stool or a chair;
I'm nae sooner doon, then aff I will flee,
To muse in the woods about Kate o' Boontree.

Aye, ance in a day I was hearty and stoot,
I'm now like a lath and as white as a cloot,
I canna live lang, and that you will see,
Unless I get married to Kate o' Boontree!

THE COURTING O' THE WIDOW.

AIR—*Lumps o' Padding.*

A BOUNCING gash widow lived up in the moors,
Ae night she sat down just to tak her four'oors,
She took a bit bite syne a sirple o' tea—
Whan down fell the saucer, and up jumpit she!
"Guid guide us," she cried, "losh, Tam, is that you?
Or is it yer ghost? hech! my heart's at my mou',
What a gliff ye ha'e gi'en me! come Tam man, sit doon,
Till I throw aff my spencer and draw on my goon."

Quo' Tam, "it's e'en me." Soon she raxed him a chair;
He took aff his bannet, syne clawed at his hair,
He glower'd, and he geck'd, and he simper'd ye ken,
For he wanted a wife like the Laird o' Cockpen.
Quo' the widow, "Come Tam man, just draw in yer
sate,
Here's a cup and a saucer, a knife and a plate,
There's a fadge and a scone, sae pit out your hand;
Poor man! your wife's dead, man, as I understand."

Quo' he, "Aye, she's gane—she is dead just a'e year;"
Now the widow look'd grand 'tween a smile and a tear!
Quo' she, "Tam, I wat, Tam, we've guid cause to
compleen,
For I've lost my Sandy and ye've lost yer Jeen."
Wi' this Tam crap near her, and thus he did say:
"I've thought about you, mem, by night and by day,
An' if ye'll consent, mem, to buckle wi' me—
Slip twa lumps o' sugar in my cup o' tea!"

The widow look'd up to the rafters aboon,
Syne she glower'd at the sugar syne play'd wi' the spoon,
Then down o'er her cheek a big tear did rin,
As her e'e fell on Tam, hech! the sugar in!
Now up frae his chair Tam jumpit wi' speed,
An' he laid his big hand on the croon o' her head,
The widow rose up an' she cried in her glee—
"Ye'll aye hae twa lumps, Tam, in your cup o' tea!"

MARY.

AIR—*There'll never be peace till Jamie comes home.*

'TWAS gloamin', the sun had gone down in the west,
And the murmuring stream hushed the woodlands to rest,
The song of the mavis had ceased for the day,
As the clouds in their beauty were fading away.
The pale silv'ry moon was ascending on high,
And the star of the evening shone bright in the sky;
By the banks of the stream, 'neath the wide-spreading tree,
My own dearest Mary came smiling to me.

With rapture I clasped my true love in my arms,
How fondly I gazed on her heavenly charms!
For her heart was as pure as an innocent dream,
And as light as the moonbeam that danced on the stream.
How sweet was the hour! O, how nameless the bliss!
How truthful our hearts, and how holy the kiss,
As down by the stream, 'neath the wide-spreading tree,
My own dearest Mary vow'd truly to me.

Now dark is the hour, how forsaken I mourn,
My love has departed—ah! ne'er to return;
Her true trusting heart lies cold in the grave,
By the banks of the stream where the willow trees wave.
In sorrow I weep, yet my weeping is vain,
No more to my bosom my darling I'll strain;
No more by the stream by the wide-spreading tree
Will my own dearest Mary come smiling to me.

LAMMERMOOR.

AIR—*Mary's Dream.*

Respectfully dedicated to Mrs. Anderson, Wyoming, Ont.

THE heather blooms upon the knowes,
Primroses spring in bielded dells,
The gowans smile on bank and brae,
Amang the blue and bonnie bells.
Down o'er the rocks the burnies fa',
They toddle on, they rin sae pure,
Through birken bowers and yellow brume
That fringe the glades in Lammermoor.

The lark sings in the lift sae blue,
The mavis sings upon the tree,
While lowly on the milk-white thorn,
The robin chirps wi' gladsome glee.
I'll never see Auld Scotland mair,
Misfortune's cloud does o'er me lour,
Nae mair I'll hear the linties' sang
Amang the hills o' Lammermoor.

Yet there in death's cold, cold embrace,
Lies ane I'll ne'er forget to lo'e,
Through weal and woe her gentle heart
To me was constant, kind, and true.
Our sindered hearts are in ae grave,
Yet I maun still my griefs endure,
By day I mourn, by night my dreams,
Are in her grave in Lammermoor.

WILLY HAS PROVED FALSE TO ME.

AIR—*Banks o' Doon.*

'TWAS in the time whan blythsome spring
Cam' smilin' after frost and snaw,
When birds were warblin' sangs o' love
On budding bough and gow'ny shaw.
When Lucy sang a mournfu' sang
Beneath yon weeping willow tree,
And aye the burden o' her sang
Was, "Willy has proved false to me."

She tore her hair wi' wild despair,
The tears rolled doon her cheeks sae pale,
'Twad break a very heart o' stane
To listen to her weary wail.
"O! Lucy, could the powers abune
Dispel the cloud that shadows thee,"
But aye the burden o' her sang
Was "Willy has proved false to me."

There is a grief nae tongue can name,
There is a tear o' deepest woe,
There is a sigh—the weary sigh—
That slighted love alane can know!
"O! Lucy, lay your hand in mine,
Yon cloud wi' silv'ry linin' see!"
But aye the burden o' her sang
Was "Willy has proved false to me."

The Trysting Nicht.

Air—*Clean Pease Strae.*

THE nicht is unco mirk and cauld,
  The snaw begins to fa';
I mickle fear that Willy, dear,
  Will ne'er can come ava.
He said he'd come—he'll strive to come,
  I'm sure he lo'es me best,
Hope beckons me aye to the door;
  Love winna let me rest!

For O! I lo'e him as my life—
  I'll lo'e him till my death;
I'm sae uplifted whan he comes
  I scarce can draw my breath!
O! come to me my Willie, dear,
  Ne'er mind the frost and snaw,
Yet far or near my heart tells me
  I lo'e ye best o' a'.

The wind roars wi' an eerie wail,
  The snaw is swirlin' sair;
A cauldriff dread creeps ower ma heart
  That I'll ne'er see him mair!
Ye angry winds, O! cease to rave,
  Ye trees to moan and sigh,
Thou moon blink in the lift abune,
  Ye blinding drifts flee by!

Sae I can hear him whistle clear,
  And see him on the lea;
That's Willie, now, I hear his step
  As sure as sure can be.
I ken it's him—that's just his rap—
  "Come Willy lad, come in;
O whisht! I doubt, that rousin' kiss
  Will wauken a' ma kin!"

I LO'E MY ALICE BEST O' A'.

AIR—*Roslin Castle.*

SWEET Nell is fair, her raven hair
  Fa's ower a neck as white as snaw,
Though Nell's divine, she'll ne'er be mine,
  I lo'e my Alice best o' a'.
In summer, down the burnside,
  When evening's shades began to fa',
How oft I've pressed her to my breast,
  And vowed I lo'ed her best o' a'.

O ! Alice thou art dear to me,
  My Alice, bonny, blyth and braw ;
Though Nellie fain my heart wad gain
  I lo'e my Alice best o' a'.
Her heart is true as heaven abune,
  My Alice has nae guile ava ;
And ilka day I vow and say,
  I lo'e my Alice best o' a'.

Though wint'ry winds are raving wild
  And loud the angry tempests blaw,
I'll o'er the hill wi' right guid will,
  And on my bonnie Alice ca'.
How soon my Alice hears my step
  As I gang round the garden wa',
And when we meet, 'tis joy complete,
  For O ! I lo'e her best o' a'.

THE ROSE OF SPRINGWELLS.

ORIGINAL AIR—*In sheet form and published by C. J. Whitney & Co., Detroit, Mich.*

HOW sweet is the spring when the soft winds are blowing,
When the cold blasts of winter have fled from the scene,
When our white-bosomed river in beauty is flowing
And nature is deck'd with her mantle of green.
How grand are thy banks, O, thou clear winding river,
When bespangled with lilies and bonny blue bells;
How oft 'mong thy groves I have wander'd with Jeannie,
My own darling Jeannie, the Rose of Springwells.
There's some may admire the sweet smile of their Marys,
And some sing the praise of their Nancy's and Nells;
But fairest, and dearest, far blythest and sweetest,
Is Jeannie, my darling sweet Rose of Springwells.

Her brow is as fair as the fairest of lilies,
And her lips are as red as the rose on the fells,
Her breath is as sweet as the zephyrs of heaven,
So pure is my Jeannie, the Rose of Springwells.
The sun may shine bright on the fairest of roses,
The birds may sing love 'mong the flow'rs of the dells
But gladness would never re-visit my bosom,
If bereft of my Jeannie, the Rose of Springwells.
There's, etc.

Away with dull care! let us banish all sorrow!
May hope be our anchor and truth be our chart,
Though fortune may frown, joy will smile on the morrow,
And undying love ever reign in the heart.

By day and by night I am thinking of Jeannie,
The bright dream of hope ever soothingly tells
That her heart is my own, and she'll aye be my darling,
My Jeannie, my joy, my sweet Rose of Springwells.
There's etc.

THE MAID OF WAYNE.

The following song is wed to a beautiful melody by M. H. McChesney, Esq., and published by Whittemore & Stephens, Detroit, Michigan.

DOWN in yon grove of maple trees,
Beside yon winding glassy rill,
Where fragrant breezes fan the air,
From scented flower and doffodill;
Beneath the shade a maiden fair
Sae blythely sang a loving strain,
The warbling birds did cease their songs,
To list the lovely Maid of Wayne.

Methought I was in fairy land,
With rapture how my heart did beat,
Methought I heard the echoes say—
No lips did ever sing so sweet.
Adown her neck the ringlets fell,
And kissed a bosom free from stain,
Her dimpled cheek and modest smile
Bespoke the lovely Maid of Wayne.

I saw her leave the grassy bank,
And lightly trip across the green,
While love among the leafy bowers
Confessed that she was nature's queen.

I saw her vanish from my sight,
  My heart can ne'er find peace again,
Enchanted I could ever gaze
  Upon the lovely Maid of Wayne.

O, were this lovely maiden mine,
  How sweetly would the moments glide;
The changing year would bring no change—
  She aye would be my winsome bride.
How I would strain her to my breast,
  But ah! the very thought is vain,
Her ardent lover lonely sighs,
  And sings the lovely Maid of Wayne.

Ellen Dear.

Published in sheet form by C. J. Whitney & Co., Detroit, Mich.

ELLEN is my apple ripe, Ellen is my pear,
  Ellen is my heart's delight, I love her a' the year;
  Ellen is my bonnie lass, fairer than the May—
  Ellen's cheek is like the rose, I love her a' the day.

When the dews o' gloamin' fa' on the budding flow'r—
Ellen's lips are sweeter far, I love her every hour.
Ellen's eyes are like the stars, fu' o' heaven's light,
Ellen is my ain true love, I love her day and night.

Some may lo'e the golden dross, some may lo'e the wine,
Some may tread the warrior's path, and some wi' tinsel shine;
Heaven grant me Ellen's love, Ellen's heart and hand,
Then I'll be, though e'er sae poor, the richest in the land.

Other lads may try to win glances frae her e'e—
Other lads can never steal my Ellen's love frae me.
When the spring comes round again, dancing in her pride,
Ellen will be a' my ain, she'll be my bonnie bride.

THE FLOWER O' DUNTROON.

Air—"Bannocks o' Barley Meal."

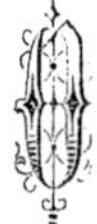

O THE hills rise sae bonnie where Lizzie resides,
And the burnie o' Battue, how sweetly it glides;
How lightsome my heart when the sun had gane doon—
As I met my ain lassie, the Flower o' Duntroon.

The west winds were rocking the pine trees to rest,
When I clasped my dear lassie wi' joy to my breast;
How truthfu' my heart, for by a' that's abune,
I vow'd to love truly the Flower o' Duntroon.

She blush'd aye sae bonnie, her eyes glanced sae clear,
When she said she'd be mine at the fa' o' the year;
How the hours fled awa; O! the mornin' cam' soon
Ere I parted frae Lizzie, the Flower o' Duntroon.

How sweet is the rose, and the violet sae blue!
And sweet is the daisy when bathed in the dew!
But the bud o' the May and the blossoms o' June
Are no' half so sweet as the Flower o' Duntroon!

The Death of McGregor.

Air—"*The Campbells are Coming.*"

GANG awa to your blankets, McGregor, my lad,
Slip awa to your blankets, McGregor, my lad,
Dinna rage round the hallan as if ye were mad,
Haud awa to your blankets, McGregor, my lad.
"Though your jo has run aff, though she's flitit her tether,
And ower the kirk-stile and awa wi' your father,
Yet ye ought to be thankfu' that she's got your dad,
Haud awa to your blankets, McGregor, my lad.

"Your vows I've nae doot were a' sealed wi' her kisses,
A fig aboot that, man, there's plenty mair lasses,
Sae cock up your beaver and no look sae sad,
Haud awa to your blankets, McGregor, my lad.
"McGregor! ye've heard 'bout the proverb nae doot,
That the fish in the sea are no a' taken out,
Man! there's haddies, and herrin', and plenty o' shad,
Haud awa to your blankets, McGregor, my lad."

We ha'e coax'd the McGregor awa to his nest;
In the howe o' the night he was greatly distress'd,
He dreamed he'd a wife wha ne'er waggit her tongue,
But wha aften cam' yerk ower his head wi' a rung.
Next moment he thought he was somebody's wife,
'Mang a hirsel o' getts wha tormented his life,
Dumfounder'd! he roared wi' a grunt and a grane—
"I'd gie my ten taes to be single again."

McGregor then tore a' his blankets in tatters,
He's rippit the bowster and smashed the bed shutters,
Unco sair he has wrestled and raged 'gainst the jad,
Wha had stolen his heart and run aff wi' his dad.
"McGregor! McGregor! losh man, will ye no
Lie still in your bed for a minit or so?"
Preserve us! he's out, and he's aff, I declare;
And the corpse o' McGregor was never seen mair!

THE AULD MAN'S COURTSHIP.

Air—"My Wife has ta'en the Gee."

NAE lad can court the bonnie lass
  Wha wons at Lammerlaw;
Her fate is sealed, she soon maun yield,
  And wed auld Daddie Ha.
Auld Daddie rode across the ford,
  Ae night at gloamin' fa';
Her mother grat, her father swat,
  When they saw Daddie Ha.

When on his shanks quo' he "what news?"
  The wife said "nane, ava,
Except our bairn, ye e'en maun learn,
  Can ne'er be Mistress Ha."
"What's that ye said?" auld Daddie cried,
  "I ga'e ye hunders twa,
And in ten days, I'll hire a chaise,
  And mak' her Mistress Ha."

"Ten days," quo' she, "losh, man alive,
  Your son has got the start;
Last night your Tam sat on the tram,
  Our daughter in the cart."
"Where did they gang?" auld Daddie cried,
  Quo' she, "across the bent."
"If sae," quo' he, "the deil tak me,
  The like o't ne'er was kent."

Auld Daddie sighed, and then replied,
  "I can nae langer tarry,
I'll e'en ride doon unto the toon,
  And notify the Shirra.

Yet weel I wat afore I gang
  Hand back the hunders twa."
Then quo' the man, "we never can,
  Tam's ta'en the gear and a.'"

Auld Daddie turned up his een,
  Syne ga'e his croon a claw;
When on his meer, he ga'e a sweer,
  And then he rode awa.
And as he rode alang the road,
  He brushed away a tear,
And faith he thought that he had bought
  His whistle unco dear.

When Nell was Aughteen.

Original Air by J. Orr Finnie, Esq., Philadelphia.

WHEN Nell was aughteen, I spak out to her mother,
She waved me away, and she said, "I wad rather
Ye'd no speak to me, but just speak to her father,
    And should he consent,
    I'm sure I'm content
That ye get your ain will o' her,
I carena though ye mak' a kirk and a mill o' her."

I gaed doon the dyke-side and confronted her father,
Quo' he, "ye daft gowk, gi'e me nane o' your blether,
To tell ye the truth, man, I carena a feather;
    Without ony fyke,
    Ye may do as ye like,
Ye may tak' your ain will o' her,
I carena though ye mak' a kirk and a mill o' her."

I gaed up the dyke-side and step'd into the kitchen,
And there I met Nell wi' her smiles sae bewitchin',
"I'm hangin'," quo' I, "like a horse in the brichin',
Your father and mother,
Ha'e gi'en their compluther,
Nell! ye needna misdoot it,
But gi'e me your hand and say nae mair aboot it."

She held out her hand, O! how fondly I pressed it,
Then her head on my shoulder how kindly it restit,
And then her affection for me she confessed it;
When the day we had fix'd,
In the week after next,
How I kissed her and clap'd her,
And swore she was mine to the end of the chapter!

I Ance Had a Lad.

Original Air by J. Orr Finnie, Esq., Philadelphia.

I ANCE had a lad was the light o' my e'e,
But now I am dowie as dowie can be,
I sit a' alane and I'm no like the lave,
Since the laddie I lo'e lies cauld in his grave.
My Minnie comes ben and she wiles me to speak,
But the wae-weary tear fa's doon o'er my cheek,
And the Laird hirples ben wi' his laugh and his leer,
To brag o' his acres, his owsen and gear.

The sigh o' my heart and the tear o' my e'e
Are dearer than a' that he's promised to me—
His words only deepen the thoughts o' regret,
For the heart that loves truly can never forget!
He fleetches and flatters to mak' me his ain,
But I'm woo'd and I'm wed to him that is gane;
The wooer wha comes when the sun's shinin' bein
Is no like the wooer wha cam' at the e'en!

THE WISDOM OF OUR FATHERS.

A SELECTION OF SCOTCH PROVERBS.

"As naething helps our happiness mair than to have the mind made up wi' right principles, I desire you, for the thriving and pleasure of you and yours, to use your een and lend your lugs to these guid *auld saws*, that shine wi' wail'd sense, and will as lang as the world wags. Gar your bairns get them by heart; let them have a place among your family books, and may never a window sole through the country be without them."—ALLAN RAMSAY.

A' are nae thieves that the dogs bark at.
A dog winna yowl if ye fell him wi' a bane.
A dry summer ne'er made a dear peck.
A bird in the hand is worth twa in the bush.
A cat may look at a king.
A dirty han' mak's a clean hearth-stane.
Ae hour's cauld will suck out seven years' heat.
A fu' purse ne'er lacks frien's.
A gangin' foot's aye gettin' (though it be but a thorn).
A guid story tells twice.
A guid name's suner tint than won.
A hungry man's an angry man.
A' complain o' want o' siller, nane o' want o' sense.
A' Stuarts are nae sib to the king.
A man may be kind an' hae little to gie.

A man is weel or wae as he thinks himsel' sae.
A misty mornin' may be a clear day.
A mou'fu' o' meat may be a townfu' o' shame.
An ill plea should be weel pled.
A nod's as guid's a wink to a blin' horse.
As broken a ship has com' to land.
As welcome as snow in hairst.
A sillerless man gangs fast through the market.
A tocherless dame sits lang at hame.
A wee bush is better than nae bield.
A wilfu' man wad need to be unco wise.
Auld sparrows are ill to tame.
A slothfu' man's a beggar's brither.
A's nae tint that's in danger.
A hasty man ne'er wanted wae.
A gi'en horse should ne'er be lookit i' the mou'.
Ae scabbet sheep spoils a' the flock.
A burnt bairn dreids the fire.
As the auld cock craws the young ane learns.
An ill shearer ne'er gat a good hook.
A guid coo may hae an ill calf.
A cock is crouse on his ain midden-head.
Ane may lead a horse to the water, but twenty winna mak' him drink.
A bonny bride's sune busket, an' a short horse is soon wispet.
A travelled man has leave to lee.
An ill life, an ill end.
Ance payed never craved.
A Scotch mist will weet an Englishman to the skin.
Ae man's meat is anither's poison.
A'thing has an' end, an' a puddin' has twa.
A new tout on an auld horn.
An idle brain's the deil's smiddy.
A' are nae maidens that wear bare hair.
A wee thing puts yer beard in a bleeze.
An ounce o' mither-wit is worth a pound o' clergy.

Auld stots ha'e stiff horns.
A sight o' you is guid for sair e'en.
Bend the back to the burden.
Better be hanged than ill married.
Better a finger aff as aye wagging.
Be a frien' to yoursel' an sae will ithers.
Beggars shouldna be choosers.
By guess, as the blin' man felled the dog.
Better a toom house than an ill tenant.
Better buy than borrow.
Better sma' fish than nane.
Better learn by your neibour's skaith than your ain skin.
Better half an' egg than a toom doup.
Bring a coo to the ha' an' she'll rin to the byre.
Be the same thing that ye wad be ca'd.
Better be alane than in ill company.
Bitin' an' scartin' is Scotch folk's wooin'.
Bannocks are better than nae kind o' bread.
Better be deid than oot o' fashion.
Chuckie stanes are ill to chow.
Chuckie stanes are nae chickens.
Come unbidden, sit unserv'd.
Comes wi' the wind an' gangs wi' the water.
Count again is nae forbidden.
Crooket carlin', quo' the cripple to his wife.
Come in and taste the tangs till the herrin's ready.
Clecking time's aye canty.
Cats are a' grey in the dark.
Dinna cast awa' the cog when the coo flings.
Do weel, an' dried nae shame.
Double drinks are good for drouth.
Drink little that ye may drink lang.
Do the likeliest, an' God will do the best.
Dirt pairts guid company.
Dummies canna lee.
Every man wishes the water to his ain mill.
Every man wears his belt his ain gate.

Every man's tale's guid till anither man's is tauld.
Every man ken's best whar his ain shoe binds him.
Either win the horse or tine the saddle.
Fat hens are ill layers.
Fear God an' keep out o' debt.
Fleyin' a bird is nae the gate to grip it.
Fules should never see half-dune wark.
Fules mak feasts, an' wise men eat them,
"An' wise men mak' proverbs, an' fules repeat them."
Fresh fish an' poor frien's grow sune ill-faur'd.
Fule's haste is nae speed.
For love o' the nurse mony ane kisses the bairn.
Fair words ne'er brak a bane, foul words may.
Far-sought and dear-bought are guid for leddies.
Fules shouldna hae chappin' sticks, nor weavers guns.
Folk should bow to the bush they get bield frae.
Feed a cauld and hunger a colic.
Fancy kills and Fancy cures.
Fleas and a girnin' wife are waukrife bedfellows.
Gang awa to yer bed, and if ye're spaired ye'll get soot to yer breakfast.
Gust yer gab wi' that an' be thankfu'.
Gar gress is ill to grow.
Gie a dog an ill name, ye may as weel hang him.
Gie him rope eneuch, an' he'll hang himsel'.
Gin *ifs* an' *ands* were pots an' pans, there wad be nae need for tinklers.
Gude folk are scarce, tak' care o' me.
Gude gear gangs intil little buik (bulk)—an' sae does poison.
Gie yer ain fish-guts to yer ain sea-maws.
Gut nae fish till ye get them.
God sen's meat, an' the deil sen's cooks.
Giff-gaff maks guid frien's.
God never strikes wi' baith han's.
God never sen's mouths but He sen's meat for them.
He's gat a hair in his neck.

He doesna ken a B frae a bull's foot.
He has nae mair mense than a miller's horse.
He hasna a leg to stand on.
He jumpit at it like a cock at a grossert.
He has licket the butter aff his bread.
Hae! gars a deaf man hear.
He wants a hair to mak a tether o'.
He should hae a lang-shaftet spune that sups kail wi' the deil.
He has feathered his nest, he may flee whan he likes.
He has crap for a' corn.
Hae ye gear, hae ye nane—tine heart an' a's gane.
He'll sune be a beggar that canna say *Na.*
He doesna aye ride when he saddles his horse.
He that cheats me ance, shame fa' *him;* he that cheats me twice, shame fa' *me.*
He that deals in dirt has aye foul fingers.
He has an e'e in his neck.
He that has a muckle nose thinks ilka ane speaks o't.
He that teaches himsel' has a fule for his maister.
His bark is waur than his bite.
He rode siccar that never fell.
Hunger is guid kitchen.
He that mayna as he wad, maun do as he may.
Hair an' hair maks the carl bare.
He that tholes overcomes.
He that winna when he may, sanna when he wad.
He ate the coo an' worried on the tail.
Hame is hame, though ever so hamely.
Hae God, hae a'.
He sits fu' still that has riven breeks.
He is at his wit's end.
He's nae sae daft as he lets on.
He counts his bawbee guid siller.
He has muckle prayer, but little devotion.
He has ae face to God an' anither to the deil.
Ilka blade o' grass keps its ain drap o' dew.

It's an ill wind that blaws naebody guid.
I hae gi'en him a stick to brak my ain head.
It's an' ill cause that a lawyer thinks shame o'.
I'll gar ye laugh at the wrang side o' yer mou.
I'll ne'er consent though yer hair was like John Harley's an' that was gowden yellow.
I winna mak fish o' ane and flesh o' another.
It wad be a hard task to follow a black soo this night through a burnt muir.
I'm o'er auld a cat to draw a strae afore.
It's hard to sit at Rome an' fecht wi' the Pope.
I wadna ca' the king my cousin.
Its an ill bird that fyles its ain nest.
If it dinna sell it winna sour.
If ye wantit me an' yer meat, ye'd want a guid frien'.
If ye brew weel ye'll drink the better ale.
Ill-doers are aye ill-dreiders.
Ill gat gear ne'er prospered.
Jouk, an' let the jaw gang by.
Keep yer tongue atween yer teeth.
Keep yer breath to cool yer broth.
Kindness canna be bought for gear.
King's caff is worth ither men's corn.
Lang looked for comes at last.
Lauchin' to haud in the greet.
Law-makers shouldna be law-breakers.
Law's costly, tak' a pint an' gree.
Lazy at meat, lazy at wark.
Like a soo playin' on a trump.
Little odds atween a feast an' a fu' wame.
Learn young, learn fair.
Like draws to like, a scabbet horse to an auld dyke.
Little gear, little care.
Live in hope and dee in despair.
Like the guidman o' Killpallet—unco simple.
Like Cranshaw kirk—as monie dogs as folk and neither room for reel or rock.

Let the tow gang wi' the bucket.
Like the tailor o' Lockermacus—ye'll drink a' the profits.
Looks as if butter wadna' melt in his mou'.
"Mair din than woo," quo' the souter whan he sheared the soo.
Maidens' bairns are aye weel bred.
Mair by luck than guid management.
Mair haste the waur speed, quo' the tailor to the lang thread.
Mak' a kirk or a mill o't.
Mak' the best o' an ill bargain.
Money mak's the mear to go.
Mony irons i' the fire—pairt maun cool.
Mony hands mak' licht wark.
Mony littles mak' a muckle.
Muckle water rins by that the miller wats na o'.
Muckle maun a guid heart thole.
Muckle head, little wit.
Nae fule like an auld fule.
Naething should be dune in a hurry but catchin' fleas.
Naething to do but cry *Fill an' fetch ben.*
Nane sae weel but he hopes to be better.
Nae plea is the best plea.
Ne'er marry a widow unless her first man was hanged.
Ne'er let on, but laugh i' yer ain sleeve.
Ne'er put a sword in a wud man's hand.
Ne'er sca'd yer lips wi' ither folk's kail.
Near the kirk may be far frae God.
Nae man has a tack o' his life.
Nearest the heart comes out first.
Nae wonder to see wasters want.
O man! an the deil war deid ye wad be chief-mourner.
Ower again's no forbidden.
Ower muckle hameliness spoils guid courtesy.
Ower muckle o' ae thing 's guid for naething.
Out o' debt, out o' danger.
Pay him hame in his ain coin.

Puir folks are glad o' broo.
Puir folks are glad o' a bellyfu' o' onything.
Pourin' water on a drooned mouse.
Pennyless sauls pine in Purgatory.
Raither spoil yer joke than tyne yer friend.
Richt wrangs nae man.
Royet lads may mak' sober men.
Rue in time.
Raise nae mair deils than ye're able to lay.
Ride the foord as ye find it.
Seein's believin', but feelin's the naked truth.
Ser' yersel', till yer bairns come o' age.
Set a stout heart to a stey brae.
Sharp stamachs mak' short graces.
Shallow waters mak' maist din.
Sma' fish are better than nane.
Speak guid o' pipers, for yer father was a fiddler.
Sudden friendship, sure repentance.
Seldom lies the deil dead at the dyke-side.
Sune eneuch if weel eneuch.
Sup awa—yer teeth are langer than yer beard.
Sair legs and ill wives should stay at hame.
Surfeits slay mair than swords.
Sue a beggar and gain a louse.
There's a teugh sinent in an auld wife's heel.
Tak' the bit an' the buffet wi't.
Tak' tent in time.
The young *may* dee, the auld *maun* dee.
The king may come in the cadger's gate.
The langest day will hae an end.
There's mony a true tale tauld in jest.
There's aye some water whar the stirkie droons.
There was ne'er eneuch whar naething was left.
They are nae a' saunts that get holy water.
Thole weed is guid for burnin'.
Tyne heart an' a's gane.
Tramp on a snail, an' she'll shoot out her horns.

The souter's wife's warst shod.
The tailor's wife's warst clad.
The langer here, the later there.
The deil's a busy bishop in his ain diocese.
The mair cost, the mair honour.
The higher up, the greater fa'.
Tak' a man by his word, an' a coo by her horn.
The grace of God is gear eneuch.
The water will ne'er warr the widdie (cheat the gallows).
There's a slippery stane at ilka bodie's door.
The maut's aboon the meal.
They'll flit in the Merse for a hen's gerse.
What is ma case the day may be yours the morn.
When prides afore, begging's ahint.
When yer gangin' and comin' the road's no empty.
Where there's heat there's reek.
Wealth mak's wit waver.
We'll ne'er ken the want o' the water till the well gangs dry.
We'll bark oursel's ere we buy dogs sae dear.
Wha daur bell the cat?
Whan ae door steeks anither opens.
Wink at wee fauts, yer ain are muckle.
Whan drink's in wit's out.
Whan the tod preaches beware o' the hens.
Wham God will help nane can hinder.
Words are but wind, but dunts are the deil.
Ye're maister o' yer ain words; but, ance spoken, yer words may maister you.
Ye canna make a silk purse o' a soo's lug.
Ye cut muckle whangs out o' ither folk's cheese.
Ye canna see wood for trees.
Ye fand it whar the Hielandman fand the tangs—at the fireside.
Ye hae tint the tongue o' your trump.
Ye hae the wrang soo by the lug.
Ye'll nae sell yer hen on a rainy day.

Ye may dicht yer neb an' flee up.
Ye ne'er saw green cheese but yer e'en reel'd.
Ye're as daft as ye're days auld.
Ye're weel awa', gin ye bide; an' we're weel quat.
Ye're sair fash'd wi' haudin' naething thegither.
Ye wad do little for God if the deil was deid.
Ye may blaw at a cauld coal.
Ye're baith simmer'd and winter'd.
Ye're just a blaw-ma-lug.
Yer looks are no yer warst fau't.
Ye've gat yer nose on the grindstone.
Ye'll neither dance or haud the can'le.
Ye'll neither hup nor wind.
Yer absence is guid company.
Yer like Rab Dale's coo—as guid as yer bonnie.
Ye ha'e a conscience like Coldingham Common.
Ye're as cross as twa sticks.
Ye're as bold as a Lammermoor Lion—*i. e.* a black-faced sheep.

GLOSSARY.

A', all
Ae, one
Aboon, above
Afore, before
Aft, often
Aften, often
Ahint, behind
Aiblins, perhaps
Aik, oak
Ain, own
Airl-penny, a coin given as earnest in hiring
Airt, direction
Ajee, ajar
Alowe, in a flame
Amang, among
An, if
Ance, once
Anither, another
Ase, ashes
Atween, between
Aucht, eight
Auld, old
Auld faurent, old fashioned
Ava, at all
Awa', away
Awmry, pantry
Awms, alms
Ayont, beyond

Bairn, a child
Bairns, children
Baith, both
Bamboozlled, stupified
Bauchels, old shoes
Bauld, bold
Bauzand, a horse or cow having a white spot on its forehead
Beck, to bow, to nod
Bein, comfortable
Beld, bald
Belyve, by and by
Ben—see but and ben
Besom, hearth-brush
Bicker, drinking vessel
Bield, shelter, refuge, protection
Bigging, building
Bike, wild bees' hive
Bing'd, curtseyed
Birr, spirit
Birried, tossed
Birrin', to throw, to run rapidly
Birkie, a young fellow
Birse, bristles
Blate, bashful
Blaw, blow
Bleare'ed, dim eyed
Blear't, bedimmed
Bleezing, blazing
Bleth'rin, talking idly
Blink, a little while, a smiling look, to look kindly, one sight
Blinking, smirking
Blythe, cheerful
Bluid, blood
Bonnie, or Bonny, handsome, beautiful
Bodin', fortelling
Bodle, or Boddle, sixth part of an English penny
Bogles, goblins
Boortree, the elder tree
Bothy, a highland cottage
Brae, side of a hill
Brat, a child
Brattle, to run
Braw, fine, handsome
Brawlie, perfectly, quite well
Bread-pan, the mouth
Breeks, breeches
Buchts, sheep pens
Buckle, marry
Bumbazed, amazed, confused
Busk, dress
Busket-braw, well dressed
But and ben, outer and inner apartment
Buffy, chubby
Burke, to choke
Burnie, streamlet
But, without
Brisket, the breast

Ca', to call, to name, to drive
Caickle, cackle
Callan, a boy
Caller, fresh, sound
Cam, come
Camstery, perverse, self-willed
Cannie, gentle, mild, dextrous
Cantie, or Canty, merry, cheerful
Cantle, crown of the head
Cantrip, incantation, spell
Carle, an old man
Carlie, a little boy
Carline, a stout old woman
Carritch, catechism
Carry, the sky
Castock, the stalk of the cabbage
Cauld, cold
Cauldriff, cold
Certie, truth
Chanter, part of a bagpipe
Chield, a young man

Chucky-staues, pebble stones
Clachan, village
Claise, or Claes, clothes
Claith, cloth
Clank, a blow
Claver, to gossip
Cleed, clothe
Cleeks, hangs
Clegs, horse flies
Clite, to fall
Clotterin', to walk awkwardly
Clout, to mend—Clout, a blow
Clour, a mark from a blow
Cluds, clouds
Cockernonie, dress cap worn by females
Coddle, to fondle
Coft, bought
Cog, a wooden dish
Coggie, a small sized wooden dish
Coost, did cast
Compluther, comply, consent
Corbie, a raven
Coup, to turn over
Couthie, kind, loving
Cowrin', cowering
Cowt, colt
Cozie, snug
Crack, to converse
Crackin', conversing
Cragie, a crag
Craik, to complain, a noise
Crap, crept
Crappen, stomach
Craws, crows
Creel, a fishwife's basket
Creepie, a low stool
Crony, comrade
Croodle, to coo as a dove
Crouse, proud
Crummie, cow
Cuif, a blockhead
Cuist, cast
Cuits, ankle bones

Dab, to peck as a bird
Daddie, a father
Daffing, funning, making sport
Daft, merry, giddy, foolish
Daidle, loiter
Daised, confused
Darg, day's work
Daud, lump
Daunder, walk slowly
Daur, dare
Daurna, dare not
Dawtie, a pet, a darling
Deave, deaf, to make a noise
Dee, die
Deeing, dying
Deftly, quickly
Delve, dig
Dern, conceal
Dibbled, planted
Ding, knock, to push
Dink, smart, tidy
Dinna, do not
Divot, a thin sod
Dochter, daughter
Doited, stupid
Donnert, stupid
Dool, sorrow, grief
Doon, down
Douce, gentle, sober, wise, prudent
Douff, pithless
Doucely, quietly
Dour, stubborn
Dover, a short sleep
Dow, or Doo, a dove
Dowie, worn with grief, sleepy
Downa, expressive of inability
Drab, a sloven
Draggin', to walk slowly
Drammach, mixture of meal and water
Drap, drop
Dree, suffer
Dreepin', dropping or wet
Droddum, the breech
Droukit, drenched
Drouth, thirst
Drumlie, muddy
Duds, clothes
Dunch, to jog with the elbow
Dunted, beat

E'e, the eye
Een, the eyes
E'enin', evening
Eerie, frightened, troubled
Eild, old age
Eldrich, fearful
En', end
Enew, enough
Ettle, to aim

Fa', fall, lot, to fall
Faes, foes
Fain, happy, fond
Fain, anxious
Farin', food
Fashious, troublesome
Fasht, troubled
Fauld, a fold, to fold
Fauts, faults
Fearfu', frightful
Fecht, to fight
Feck, most part
Fee, hire
Fen, to make shift
Ferlies, wonders
Fidging, uneasy
Fient, fiend
Fitfa', footfall
Fistle, bustle
Flaffer, flutter
Flee, fly
Fleech, to supplicate, to coax
Forbye, besides
Forgie, to forgive
Forjesket, tired, wearied
Fou, full, tipsy
Foumart, a fox
Fouth, lots
Frae, from
Fuffin', puffing
Fu', full
Funk, to kick
Fyke, restlessness

Gab, the mouth, to speak boldly or pertly
Gabbing, speaking and chatting
Gae, to go
Gaed, went
Gaen, or Gane, gone
Gaet, or Gate, way, manner, road
Gaffaw, loud laughter
Gang, to go, to walk
Gar, to make, to force
Gart, made
Gaucy, jolly, large
Gaun, going
Gauntrees, frames on which casks are placed
Gawky, foolish, romping
Gear, riches, goods of any kind
Gee, pet
Gerse, grass
Ghaist, a ghost
Gie, to give
Girning, grinning
Gied, gave
Gien, given
Gilpey, half-grown, halt informed boy or girl
Gin, if, against
Glaiket, foolish, mad
Glamour, the influence of a charm
Glaur, mud
Gled, a hawk
Gleg, quick, clear-sighted
Glint, glance
Glisk, glimpse
Gloamin', twilight
Glow'r, to stare, to look
Glunch, frown, gloom
Gomeril, a fool
Goupins, handfuls
Goustie, ghostly
Gowan, mountain or field daisy
Gowd, gold
Gowk, fool
Grannie, grandmother
Grane, groan
Grat, wept
Gree, pre-eminence
Greetin', crying, weeping
Grien, to wish, covet
Grit, great
Gript, grasped
Grop, to feel
Growl, snarl, discontent
Grue, shudder
Grup, grip
Gude, good
Guid e'en, good evening
Guid-mornin', good morning
Guidman and Guidwife, the master and mistress of the house
Guidfather and Guidmother, the father-in-law and mother-in-law
Gutcher, grandsire

Ha', hall
Hae, to have
Haen, had
Hale, whole
Hairst, harvest
Halesome, wholesome
Hallan, cottage
Hallanshaker, a scamp who stands shaking in the hallan, a stout beggar man
Hame, home
Haffits, sides of the head
Haflins, the half
Hantle, great deal
Hap, to shield, to cover up
Harum scarum, half-mad
Haugh, a low flat piece of land
Haud, hold
Hear't, hear it
Haver, to talk foolishly
Hech! oh, strange
Heich, high
Herrin', herring
Hinney, honey
Hirple, to walk lame
Hizzie, romping girl
Hotch, jolt, shake
Hoodie-craw, a raven
Hool, husk
Howdie, a midwife
Howket, dug
Howlet, owl
Hurklin, cowering

Ilk, each
Ilka, every
Ingle, fire-place
Ingleside, fireside
I'se, I shall or will
Ither, other, one another

Jag, prick
Jaunt, a journey
Jaupit, bespattered
Jaw, raillery, wave
Jee, change
Jink, to dodge, to turn suddenly round a corner
Jo, sweetheart
Jouk, stoop down
Joyfu', joyful

Kail-yard, cabbage garden
Kame, comb
Kebbuck, a cheese
Keek, look, a peep, to peep
Keeking-glass, looking-glass
Kelpies, evil spirits haunting streams
Kempin', striving
Ken, to know
Kend, or Kent, knew
Kenna, know not
Kens, knows
Keps, catches
Kilt, a portion of the highland garb
Kimmer, a gossip
Kin, kindred, relations
Kirn, a churn, the harvest supper
Kirsen, christen or baptize
Kist, chest
Kittle, to tickle, ticklish
Knowe, a small round hillock
Kye, cows

Kyloes, black Highland cattle
Kyte, the belly

Laddie, a boy, diminutive of lad
Laigh, low
Laith, unwilling
Lane, lone—My lane, myself, alone
Lanely, lonely
Lang, long, to think long, to long, to weary
Lamping, to take long steps
Lap, leap
Lauch, laugh
Lave, the rest, the remainder, the others
Laverock, the lark
Law, low
Leal, true
Lee, an untruth
Lee lang, live long
Leeze me, a phrase of congratulation, I am happy in thee, or proud of thee
Leg-bail, run off
Leugh, laugh
Leuk, a look, to look
Licht, light
Lift, sky
Lightlie, despise
Lilt, a ballad, a tune, to sing
Lilting, singing
Limmer, an abandoned female
Linn, a waterfall, or the pool at the bottom of it
Lintie, linnet
Loaning, a broad lane
Lo'e, love
Lo'ed, loved
Loof, the palm of your hand
Loon, a wild young lad
Loot, did let
Losin, a pane of glass
Lounder, to strike
Loup, leap
Lugs, ears
Lyart, old, thin
Lowe, flame

Mae, more
Mak', make
Mailin, farm
Mair, more
Maist, most
Maistly, mostly
Maukin, a hare
Maun, must
Maunna, must not
Mark, a Scottish coin
Marrow, equal, like
Mauled, to strike repeatedly
Mavis, the thrush
Mense, manners
Merse, a portion of Berwickshire
Mess John, the minister
Micht, might
Minnie, mother
Mirk, dark
Mischanter, misfortune
Mither, mother
Monnie, or mony, many

Mou', mouth
Moudiwart, a mole
Muckle, or Mickle, great, big much
Mutch, cap worn by females
Mutchkin, English pint
Mysel', myself

Na, no, not
Nae, no, not any
Naething, or Naithing, nothing
Naig, a nag or horse
Naigies, horses
Nane, none
Neivefu', handful
Neist, next
Nicht, night
Nicker, to neigh
Niff-naff, fastidious
Nippin, piercing, pinching
Nippit, pinched
Nocket, lunch
Nook, corner
Noucht, nought
Nout-horn, cow-horn
Nowte, cattle

O', of
O'ercome, burden, as of a song
Onie, any
O't, of it
Oursels, ourselves
Owre, often, too
Owsen, oxen
Oxtering, to link arms

Paiks, knocks
Pairtin', parting
Palaver, hypocritical talk
Pawky, sly or cunning
Pechin', breathing hard
Perlins, jewels
Philabeg, the kilt
Pibroch, pipe, tune
Pickle, a small quantity
Pingle, to mop
Pirn, a spool
Plack, an old Scottish coin
Pliskie, to trick
Pouch, pocket
Pouther'd, powdered
Pow, head
Pree, to taste
Pree'd, tasted
Pu'd, pulled
Puirtith, poverty
Puir, poor

Quo, said

Rackle-handed, strong-handed
Raid, inroad, foray
Rampageous, raging, prancing
Rang, reigned
Rax, fetch, reach
Rede, warn
Reek, smoke
Rifted, torn
Rin, run
Ristle, to strike

Rout, the blowing of a horn
Routh, plenty
Rowans, berries of the mountain ash
Rowpit, hoarse
Rubbit, rubbed
Rung, a walking stick

Sae, so
Saft, soft
Sair, sore
Sairly, sorely
Sang, song
Sark, shirt
Sassenach, Saxon or Lowlander
Scaur, a steep bank
Scraughin', screaming
Screed, to lecture
Scrivein', to go swiftly
Scunner, disgust
Sel', self
Shank, to depart or set off. a thin scranky leg, a handle
Shauchled, ill or loosely shaped
Shaw, a wood in a hollow place
Shearing, reaping
Sheiling, cot, a cottage
Shill, shrill
Shindie, disturbance
Shorking, wet feet
Sic, such
Siccan, such
Sicker, keen
Siller, silver money
Simmer, summer
Sin', since
Skaith, to damage, to injure, injury
Skeigh, proud, nice, high mettled
Skelly, to squint
Skelp, to strike, to walk with a smart tripping step
Skirling, shrieking, crying
Skreigh, a scream, to scream
Slaw, slow, dull
Slee, sly
Sleekit, sleek, sly
Slogan, cry, war cry
Sma,' small
Smack, kiss
Smeddum, strong, active
Smoored, smothered
Snaw, snow, to snow
Snawy-drift, snow-drift
Sneeshin', snuff
Sonsy, stout, good looking
Sough, the sighing of the wind
Souse, to plunge, dip
Spak', spake
Speel'd, clamb
Speir, ask
Speired, inquired
Spence, parlor
Splarge, splutter
Sprachlin', scrambling
Spurtle, a stick with which porridge is stirred when boiling
Stane, stone
Stancy, stoney
Stappit, stepped
Starn, or Sternie, a star
Steek, shut
Stended, strided or walked
Stots, oxen
Stoun, pang
Stoups, measures for holding liquids
Stour, dust
Stown, stolen
Stracvaget, to go idlely
Sumph, fool
Sunkets, left meats
Swarf, fright
Swarf, swoon
Swatter, splutter, flounce
Sweirt, not caring
Syne, then

Taen, taken
Tak', to take
Takin', taking
Tak'tent, take heed
Tane, tother, the one, the other
Tapsalteerie, upside down
Tent, caution, to take heed
Thae, these
Thegither, together
Thole, suffer, require, endure
Thowless, cold, broken-hearted
Thrapple, the throat
Thraws, turns
Tine, to lose
Tings, tongs
Tint, lost
Tither, the other
Titterin', giggling
Tittie, sister
Tittlen, to whisper
Tocher, marriage portion
Toddlin, tottering
Toom, empty
Totting, a child's run
Tousie, disordered, hair uncombed
Trig, spruce, neat
Trow, believe, know
Tryst, a meeting by appointment
Twa, two
Tyke, dog
Tyne, lose

Unco, strange
Uncouth, uncomely
Usqueba, a kind of whisky

Wa', wall
Wad, would
Waddin', wedding
Wadna, would not
Wae, sorrowful
Waefu', wailing, woeful
Waes, woes
Wair, to lay out, to expend
Wallop, to leap, strike
Walth, plenty
Wark, work
Warlock, wizard
Warst, worst
Warstle, wrestle
Wat-ye, know ye
Waukin', waking
Waukrife, sleepless

Waur, worse
Wean, child
Weary, or Wearie, tired
Wede, weeded
Wee, little
Weel, well
Weelfare, welfare
Weel waled, well chosen
Ween, a vow—I ween, I wot
Weet, rain, wetness, dew
Weir, war
Weird, destiny
We'se, we shall
Wha, who
Wha'll, who will
Wha wadna, who would not
Whack, to fall, to strike
Whang, to cut
Whare, where
Whiff, to fly off
Whilk, which
Whingin', to whine
Whisht, silence
Whisket, brushed past
Whuds, runs nimbly
Whummlin', to turn over
Whup, with
Wi', with
Willows, baskets
Wimple, meandering of a brook, a curl, undulation
Winna, will not
Winsome, hearty, gay
Wizend, wrinkled, withered, dried up
Woo', wool
Woo, to court, to make love
Wraith, an apparition exactly like a living person, the appearance of which is said to forebode the person's death
Wrang, wrong, to wrong
Wud, mad, distracted
Wull cat, wild cat
Wylie, cautious
Wyte, blame

Yade, pony
Yaff, chat, bark like a dog
Yammer, to grumble
Yatter, senseless talk
Ye'll, you will
Yerk, to strike
Ye'se, you shall
Yestreen, last night
Yett, gate
Ye've, ye have
Yird, earth
Yoursel', yourself
Youthfu', youthful
Yule, Christmas

www.ingramcontent.com/pod-product-compliance
Lightning Source LLC
LaVergne TN
LVHW011222110826
845150LV00006B/1516

* 9 7 8 1 4 2 5 5 1 5 3 5 5 *